Searching Electronic Resources

Second Edition

By Marjorie L. Pappas, Gayle A. Geitgey, athy A. Jefferson

PROFESSIONAL GROWTH SERIES®

A Publication of THE BOOK REPORT & LIBRARY TALK
Professional Growth Series

Linworth Publishing, Inc.
Worthington, Ohio

Published by Linworth Publishing, Inc.
480 East Wilson Bridge Road, Suite L
Worthington, Ohio 43085

Series Information:

From The Professional Growth Series

ISBN 0-938865-67-6

5 4 3 2 1

Table of Contents

ACKNOWLEDGEMENTS

Follett Software has granted permission for this use of the
Pathways to Knowledge ™ Model

The authors wish to thank their families, friends, and colleagues for their encouragement and support during the creation of this book.

Windows is a trademark of Microsoft Corporation

ABOUT THE AUTHORS

Marjorie L. Pappas, Ph. D. is an associate professor and Coordinator of the Division of School Library Media Studies at The University of Northern Iowa, in Cedar Falls, where she has taught courses in Research, Computer Applications, and Information Skills.

Gayle A. Geitgey is the district and high school library media specialist in the Urbana City Schools, Ohio, where she partners with teachers to develop unites that reflect resource-based learning and the integration of information skills. Gayle is an adjunct instructor for Wright State University, Dayton, Ohio, where she presents a workshop on young adult literature and information skills.

Cathy A. Jefferson is the high school technology coordinator for Centerville City Schools, Ohio, where she assists the district technology coordinator in implementing the district's technology needs. She is also an adjunct instructor for the Department of Education, Wright State University, Dayton.

Introduction

Background Information

Electronic information resources are being developed at an astonishing rate today. Library media specialists (LMS), teachers, and students have an exciting array of electronic resources available on CD-ROM and the Web, which present a new set of challenges for accessing information. Some of these electronic resources are clearly informational and could be compared to both the reference and nonfiction books in a library media center. For example, the *Compton's Encyclopedia* is now available in electronic format as the *Compton's Interactive Encyclopedia* (The Learning Company). Others, dubbed electrobooks, often are fiction stories and picture books with interactivity options. These options can engage students in hyperlinked selections that sometimes enhance the story, or influence the story outcome. *Just Grandma and Me* (Broderbund) shows the story text on the screen along with Mercer Mayer's illustrations. Students can select one of two options: listen to an auditory version of the story while watching illustrations on the computer's monitor; or listen to the auditory version and then select parts of each illustration, known as hotspots, that are animated and provide additional elements of the story.

A growing number of electrobooks are being produced as interactive browsers. These books are informational but few include a search engine, which is a software feature that enables the user to systematically locate information using procedures that search across text. Access to information is through hyperlinked connections, a linking process using buttons or hotspots that enable a user to move through the electrobook in a nonlinear manner. *I, Leonardo* (Interactive Publishing) presents information about Leonardo DaVinci's life using pictures, drawings, and multimedia clips, with audio narration. Users of this CD-ROM disc can click on buttons and make hyperlinked connections about interesting events in DaVinci's life which represents an Explore Search strategy. However, this disc has no search engine, so a student cannot pursue a Browse, Analytical or Hierarchical search strategy.

Many electronic information resources have features that enable formal search strategies, with functions that search subject or title lists, subjects based on a hierarchical structure, and full or defined text. These resources are exciting because they enable access to information that is nonlinear (as opposed to the linear access in paper books) and the full text or keyword searching capability avoids the frustrations searchers often encountered with subject searching that uses a formal and stylized vocabulary. Accessing information that is available in a nonlinear format allows a student to explore relationships and make connections that sometimes happen in a serendipitous manner. Although this means teachers and LMS have wonderful new resources available, they are faced with the challenge of learning that these resources have very different screen designs and searching software, a process which can be frustrating and confusing. Different formats, such as Macintosh, DOS, and Windows add to the confusion. Books and periodicals have consistent formats, but this is not the case with electronic information resources. LMS must be able to provide new users of electronic resources with basic search strategies that they can use easily as they move from one resource to another.

The primary electronic information resource format represented in this book is CD-ROM. A limited number of Web-based electronic resources are included, e.g. *Britannica*

Online, Electric Library. When CD-ROM resources have a Web connection these are noted in the description area of the Search Strategy Form.

This book provides LMS and teachers with four basic search strategies that are available in most electronic resources:

- Explore Search
- Browse Search
- Hierarchical Search
- Analytical Search.

These strategies are part of *Pathways to Knowledge ™: Follett's Information Skills Model* (Pappas & Tepe, 1997) that presents a nonlinear information process model as a graphical representation.

This book also provides teachers and LMS with a tool to enable students to become independent users of electronic resources. The notions of resource-based teaching and student-centered learning put students into an active information-seeking role. Managing this type of learning environment is a challenge for teachers as their students move in many directions pursuing their projects. Students often need to use resources in small groups or independently. This challenges teachers and LMS to be available as coaches and facilitators. Providing students with graphic organizers and self-help information are effective management strategies.

Organization

This book has been developed and organized with two audiences in mind. Chapters One to Three were written to provide the LMS or teacher information about the Pathways Model and the specific search strategies for individual electronic resources on the Search Strategy Forms. Chapter Four includes individual Search Strategy Forms that provide concise instructions for using the search strategies of Explore, Browse, Hierarchical, and Analytical with specific electronic resources. Here we consider students as the primary audience.

The Search Strategy Forms are presented in a horizontal format so that LMS and teachers can photocopy and use them next to computer workstations.

Getting Started

The authors' primary goal was to limit the Search Strategy Form to one page with concise information focused at the beginning level. Thus, it was not possible to include every detail of the search features within each electronic resource. A further challenge was to provide sufficient detail to get students started without too many instructions. As new versions of the electronic resource become available, procedures may change. All users are cautioned to check their version against the version indicated on the form as all information may not be accurate with updates.

Teachers and LMS are encouraged to suggest students follow a holistic process as they gather and use information. For example, some Presearch activities will help students use their prior knowledge to identify keywords for searching electronic resources. The section on the Pathways Model provides more detail on this process.

As students begin to use the Search Strategy Forms, they may need initial guidance in opening the software. This process varies greatly from one system to another and is influenced by whether the software is loaded on a network or running on a stand-alone workstation. It may be helpful to create a software instruction form to accompany the Search Strategy Form.

Using the Search Strategy Forms

The Search Strategy Forms include bibliographic and descriptive information about the electronic resource in the top section of each form. The descriptive information includes these levels: preschool-kindergarten (P-K), elementary (E), middle school or junior high (M-J), senior high (S) and adult (A). Information regarding Help, Note taking, and Printing is included below the bibliographic information. Help is an important feature in electronic resources today when the focus is on enabling students as independent searchers. Students should be encouraged to use the Help feature before asking others. Software includes many Help functions available in context. For example, if a searcher is having difficulty while trying to print an encyclopedia article and selects Help from the Menu, the section on Printing should appear on the screen.

A growing number of electronic resources include a Note taking feature and students should be encouraged to use this whenever possible. Typically, students can copy sections of text and paste them into an electronic notepad. This notepad can be saved to their own disk and opened later in a computer lab using a word processor. As students develop their notes electronically, they should be required to include the appropriate bibliographic citation for summary information and quotations. Most electronic resources permit text Note taking. As more graphics and illustrations are added to electronic resources, students will be able to add electronic copies to their notes. Because graphics often convey a message not always included in the text, students may need to copy graphics to adequately present a concept or idea.

Printing allows students to leave the workstation with a hard copy of their research information. Print functions differ across the many electronic resources, so this has been included as another significant feature. As with Note taking, a growing number of electronic resources allow the printing of both text and graphics.

The lower section of the Search Strategy Form includes columns that describe the specific features for Explore, Browse, Hierarchical, and Analytical Searches within each resource. Not all electronic resources contain the features that enable all of the four search strategies, and when this occurs, the phrase Not Available appears in the column. Explore and Browse Searching tend to be the easiest strategies to start an initial entry into the electronic resource, so teachers and LMS may encourage students to begin their search in this way.

Chapter One: Pathways to Knowledge™ and Electronic Searching

As electronic information resources (CD-ROM & Internet) replace print resources in school library media centers and appear on classroom workstations, teachers and library media specialists (LMS) need to teach students to use these resources. This instruction is a part of information skills and many LMS use an information process model as their framework. When students need to use an electronic information resource often the LMS may begin by instructing students on the use of CD-ROM or Internet resource. Although this activity may encourage students to search for information, this instruction occurs without any connection to a holistic information seeking process. This chapter explores one information process model, *Pathways to Knowledge™* (Pappas and Tepe, 1997) with a focus on using electronic information resources.

Pathways to Knowledge™

The Pathways Model located at the end of this chapter illustrates an information process that includes the following stages:

- Appreciation
- Presearch
- Search
- Interpretation
- Communication
- Evaluation.

These stages provide students with a menu of strategies to apply as they gather, evaluate and use information. Students are encouraged to select the appropriate stage and strategy as their information needs require.

Appreciation

Many electronic information resources contain features which teachers might use for appreciation activities. The Pathways Model provides the following definition of the Appreciation stage:

> *Individuals appreciate literature, the arts, nature and information in the world around them through varied and multiple formats, including stories, film, paintings, natural settings, music, books, periodicals, the Web, video, etc. Appreciation often fosters curiosity*

and imagination, which can be a prelude to a discovery phase in an information seeking activity. As learners proceed through the stages of information seeking their appreciation grows and matures throughout the process. (Pappas & Tepe, 1997)

Literary appreciation is an important part of the language arts and reading curriculum. Teachers and LMS engage students in many activities that develop their enjoyment of stories through books, videos, or storytelling. These activities foster a sense of curiosity that causes students to seek additional information. For some students, this is the beginning of their information seeking process, rather like dropping a pebble in the pond and watching the ripples become ever-increasing concentric circles.

Appreciation becomes, for some searchers, their initial Pathways stage. However, teachers and LMS need to help students understand that this stage is related to other stages of the Pathways Model. Too often students feel their research activities lead only to a formal paper. They need to understand that their discovery activities are a legitimate part of an information seeking process.

Presearch

The Presearch stage encourages students to establish their focus by developing an overview and exploring relationships. The Pathways Model provides the following definition of Presearch:

The Presearch stage enables searchers to make a connection between their topic and prior knowledge. They may begin by brainstorming a web or questions that focus on what they know about their topic and what they want to know. This process may require them to engage in exploratory searching through general sources to develop a broad overview of their topic and explore the relationships among subtopics. Presearch provides searchers with strategies to narrow their focus and develop specific questions or define information needs. (Pappas & Tepe, 1997)

Typically, students will be more efficient at searches if they develop an overview of their topic using a Presearch strategy. This important stage of the information seeking process is often ignored. The teacher or LMS should act as a facilitator, providing activities and discussion to help students relate the topic to their prior knowledge and build background information. One strategy might include a brainstorming session using a web to explore relationships between topics. Sometimes this discussion alone will enable students to identify key words that effectively frame the topic and that might be used for searching. In other cases, where students may have little knowledge of the topic, the brainstorming session may not generate enough information to develop an overview.

When students lack sufficient topic information for a broad overview, teachers can suggest they explore the library media center's general resources, for example, encyclopedias, yearbooks, almanacs, handbooks, etc. Electronic encyclopedias are particularly useful here because the search features allow students to explore and make hyperlink connections without developing a formal search strategy. Media specialists and teachers can encourage students to add related topics to their web as their information expands. Once they have enough background information, they can more easily develop specific research questions or define an information need.

Search

The Search stage of the Pathways Model is important because students focus on pursuing planned strategies rather than a haphazard use of specific resources. The Pathways Model provides the following definition of Search:

> *During the Search stage, searchers identify appropriate information providers, resources and tools, then plan and implement a search strategy to find information relevant to their research question or information need. Searchers are open to using print and electronic tools and resources, cooperative searching and interaction with experts.* (Pappas & Tepe, 1997)

In today's information-rich environment, students learn to select from a variety of information resources and formats. As the emphasis on authentic projects expands, students must recognize that information may come from interviewing a local expert; or accessing a Web site on the Internet; or reading a book at the library media center. In the Search stage students plan and implement their search strategy by identifying information providers, selecting information resources and tools, and seeking relevant information.

Electronic tools and resources have common features, which allow students to apply specific search strategies. These common features and related search strategies represent a framework or recipe which can be applied by students once they know what to look for and these skills will serve them across resources and hardware environments.

The specific search strategies on the Pathways Model are:

- *Explore Search* (looking, surfing, hyperlinking with a general topic)
- *Browse Search* (examining a linear list or index by topic)
- *Hierarchical Search* (examining a body of knowledge from a broad concept to a specific topic)
- *Analytical Search* (electronically searching specified or full text using keyword,

Boolean, concept search, etc.) (Pappas & Tepe, 1997)

Explore Search

Students use an Explore Search when they are in a discovery mode or unsure of a specific topic for a project. Explore Searching can be applied by students whether they are using electronic resources or paper. Flipping through the pages of a magazine, or looking at books on a shelf, or surfing the Web is an Explore Search.

In an electronic resource, students often surf the Web or CD-ROM software, selecting hot spots or buttons that hyperlink to other topics. This form of searching is a serendipitous or free form method of looking for information. An Explore Search does not require a planned strategy, but does enable the searcher to connect topics or concepts with related topics in a nonlinear manner. Various electronic resources enable this hyperlinking feature sometimes using buttons or icons.

For example, a searcher has found an article on *Mound Builders*. In the text, the phrase *Serpent Mound* is displayed in blue, rather than black text. Using the mouse, the searcher could position the cursor over the phrase and press the mouse button. A new screen appears with information on the *Serpent Mound*. A hypertext connection has been made and the student is Explore Searching.

Browse Search

Many electronic information resources have a Browse Search feature. Typically a list of subject words or article titles generate a linear list much like an index in a paper resource. When the searcher selects a word or title, the software opens the full text of the article. A Browse Search is useful to a searcher who is just beginning to look for information on a topic, because little or no search strategy is required. It is important for searchers to understand that a browse search feature in software looks through a list of subject words or titles but does not search through the full text.

To begin a Browse Search, the searcher should examine the options on the Menu Bar or Tool Bar for features like Title List, Contents, or Browse. Selecting this feature will typically display a list of titles or subjects and a dialog box. The searcher types a search word and the software highlights that word if it is available. If not, the program may indicate where the word would have appeared were it on the list. The searcher can then see other related list words that provide options for accessing information on the same topic.

For example, a searcher is looking for information on *fire*. She selects Subject List from the Menu Bar and an alphabetical list of subjects appears on the screen. A dialog box appears at the top of the screen and the searcher types in *fire*. The software displays the subject list, which is close to, or matching, the word *fire*. If the word *fire* appears in the list, the searcher can select this word and the article about *fire* appears on the screen. If the word *fire* is not in the list, similar words, like *fire alarm*, *fire ant*, *fire engine* or *fireplace* may appear. This strategy enables the searcher to begin locating information in the resource.

Hierarchical Search

Electronic information resources include a hierarchical feature often labeled Subject Tree, Knowledge Tree, Topic Tree, or Categories, which organizes information from a broad concept to a specific topic. This feature allows students to do a Hierarchical Search, which is useful, because it requires only a limited understanding of the search topic and no planned strategy. A Hierarchical Search is similar to classifying. To do a Hierarchical Search students select from a list of general topics or concepts. The Hierarchical strategy engages searchers in topic selections that move from the general to the specific. This selection produces another list of topics. Each additional selection produces a more narrowly defined list of topics until a list of specific articles appears.

The *Grolier Multimedia Encyclopedia* provides one of the best examples of a Hierarchical Search feature with their *Knowledge Tree*. When students select the *Knowledge Tree*, a list of broad concepts appears, e.g. *geography, history, science,* etc. Selection of a concept opens another box with more specific concepts or words related to the students' search topic. This process is repeated until a list of articles appears.

For example, a student searching for information on *light* might begin by selecting the hierarchical feature button. The next screen includes a list of general disciplines or concepts. The student selects *science,* because *light* is a topic within the science class. The next screen contains a list of general science topics, and the student selects *physics.* The student continues to make selections like *waves and wave motion,* and *electromagnetic waves,* until *light* appears on the list. The student selects this topic and the next screen contains information about *light.* In some cases, the search topic will not be included on the final list. That may occur because the electronic resource contains no information on the topic; or, it may be that the searcher began the Hierarchical Search by selecting the wrong topic or concept. Before moving to another search strategy, the searcher might re-examine his topic selections from each list and consider different choices or a different starting point. Some electronic resources provide a screen display showing the hierarchical progression of topic selections made by a searcher. *The Grolier Multimedia Encyclopedia* provides an excellent example of this type of display, which makes it a useful example for teachers and students about a Hierarchical Search.

A Hierarchical Search is particularly useful for a student who has a general topic to research but little or no information about the scope of her topic. A Hierarchical Search will give the student a broad perspective and visually illustrate the manner in which a topic is related to other topics.

Analytical Search

Analytical search features in electronic resources look for a specific word or phrase searching through full or defined text. These search features might be labeled Search, Find, Keyword, or Topic and are part of the software search engine. Many analytical search features include a simple and complex search option. A simple search allows students to enter a word or phrase but does not provide for the use of Boolean operators. A complex search uses Boolean operators.

Many electronic resources have a search engine that uses the Boolean operators, AND, OR, and NOT. When resources use WITH (AND) and WITHOUT (NOT), the opening default choice is OR. These operators allow a searcher to combine words to either narrow or broaden a topic.

Boolean Operators

The operator OR will broaden a topic causing the software to search for either word in the dialog box. With the use of this operator, it is not necessary for both words to be present in an article or citation for the software to identify a hit. Thus the list of hits is larger than the number of hits identified when AND or NOT is used.

For example, a searcher may use the operator OR, with the search phrase, *pollution* OR *acid rain*. The software identifies any article or citation that contains either the words *pollution* or *acid rain*.

The Boolean operator AND is used to combine words or phrases. It initiates a search through full text or citations for information that reflects both words or phrases. A search using AND produces a more narrowly constrained list of hits because both words must be present in the text or citation before the software identifies a hit.

For example, a searcher looking for information on *pollution* who has identified *acid rain* as a related concept may enter the search phrase *pollution* AND *acid rain* in the dialog box. This search requires the software to identify articles or citations that contain both the word *pollution* and the phrase *acid rain*.

The Boolean operator NOT is used to eliminate a word or phrase from a search. This type of search strategy directs the software to search for a word, but not include text about a related word.

For example, the searcher may be interested in information related to *pollution* AND *acid rain*, but only as these occur in the *United States*. In this case, the searcher might use the operator NOT, with the following search phrase, *pollution* AND *acid rain* NOT *Canada*, in the dialog box.

Such a search phrase tells the software to combine the words *pollution* and *acid rain*, but eliminate those references, which include the word *Canada*. Searchers are cautioned to use the Boolean operator NOT with care because such a restriction may eliminate articles or text relevant to the search.

Searchers are cautioned to consider the resource being searched as they plan their search strategy. Search phrases that contain multiple Boolean operators may be less productive in resources where full-text is not present, such as electronic catalogs or citation-only periodical indexes. These resources contain fewer searchable words than a full-text resource.

Using Truncation, Proximity, and Wild Cards

Other features that can focus a search include truncation, proximity, and wild cards. These features are often software specific so they are discussed here only in a generic sense. Teachers and LMS are encouraged to check electronic resources for specific instructions.

Truncation involves identifying the root or base spelling of a word and using a symbol to instruct the software to search for all forms of the word which contain that base spelling. For example, if a searcher were looking for information on *libraries*, several words might lead to information on this topic and they all begin with the base spelling of *librar*. If the software searches for all the words that begin with this base word, it might identify *libraries*, *librarian*, and *library*. Many electronic resources require the searcher to put an asterisk (*) as the final character in a truncated word, so the word would be entered in the dialog box as: *librar**. Some electronic resources may use another symbol.

Wild card options are used less frequently, but enable a search for words that have variant spelling. For example: *man* or *men*; *woman* or *women*. If words similar to these are used in a search phrase, the searcher might use a wild card to instruct the software to search for both forms of the word. That search phrase would be entered in the dialog box in this manner:

M?n.

The symbol, ?, is a code the software recognizes to search for words that contain the letters *m* and *n* with different letters between. Not all electronic resources have this feature, but use of the operator OR would accomplish the same objective, e.g. *men* OR *man* and *women* OR *woman*.

Proximity relates to the parameters or rules that electronic resources establish for the distance or the spatial relationship of words used in a search statement. Since types of proximity tend to be very software specific, this discussion is rather general.

One proximity issue occurs when a phrase rather than a word is used in the dialog box. In some electronic resources, a phrase in the search statement must be enclosed in quotation marks or the software presumes each word in the phrase is connected with an AND, which will greatly alter the search results. This is more likely to occur when the dialog box is only one rectangle on the screen. When there are multiple dialog boxes, connected by Boolean operators positioned outside each box, the software presumes words entered within each separate dialog box are connected phrases. Another proximity type occurs when it is possible to instruct the software to search for words in the same sentence, or within a paragraph or an article. The default option might be a paragraph, but changing this proximity option will influence the results of the search. Sometimes the setup option will allow a searcher to select the number of words between the words of a phrase. The default might be 50 words apart. Changing this setting to 15 words apart would narrow the search. Typically, the closer in proximity words are to each other in text, the greater the chance the article has relevance to the chosen topic.

Concept searching is a feature available in some electronic resources. A concept search allows a student to input a phrase or sentence into the dialog box but does not use Boolean operators. The software uses probability to expand the search to other words which have relevance to those used in the phrase or sentence.

Determining Relevancy

Determining relevancy is an important strategy in this age of information overload. Students establish the relevancy of information by checking for accuracy, currency, or whether the information is fact or fiction. It is also important for students to distinguish between a primary or secondary source of information.

Students often want to print an entire article from an electronic resource, which ties up a workstation for long periods of time. If time and workstation availability permits, this allows a useful relevancy strategy. Students can use the hard copy of their information and a highlighter to identify the parts of the text that are inaccurate, obsolete, or fiction rather than established facts. If there is only one workstation in the LMC, printing the article may not be the most expedient way of providing a class of students with their turn on the electronic encyclopedia. Some teachers have solved this problem by suggesting that students construct an electronic notes file of summarized comments and quotes from the text or extensive parts of the article, then saving to their floppy disks. Students can open a word processor in the computer lab and filtering strategies can occur there, leaving the electronic resource workstation available for other searchers.

Note taking

As students gather information, they need a system of Note taking and frequently teachers have suggested they use the strategy of note cards. Electronic resources often have Note taking features that enhance the Note taking process, and some of these are full-function word processors. Electronic Note taking features mesh with other software applications available today and students should be strongly encouraged to use them. For example, many electronic encyclopedias have a notes feature in which students may store relevant passages of text. Notes features act as simple word processors, permitting students to develop their own summary and synthesis of the encyclopedic information. Because of the concern of plagiarism, instructors must encourage students to summarize, paraphrase, and quote with appropriate citations. Teachers may provide students with formats for citation references and indicate they should be constructed when students copy text from the encyclopedia to their notes file. Teachers should peruse electronic notes frequently and if the appropriate citations are missing, direct students to return to the electronic resource to locate and record the citation information.

Another aspect of Note taking is using text versus graphic information in electronic resources. We tend to assume that "notes" are synonymous with "text," but in the electronic environment this is not necessarily the case. There is a growing quantity of visual information representation within electronic resources and students need the ability to replicate or represent this information in their notes. Many electronic resources provide a function for printing both text and visuals and students should be encouraged to incorporate these visuals into their notes and ultimately within their completed project, along with the appropriate reference citations. The optimum way to include this visual information is to copy and paste the visual electronically and then integrate the appropriate visual into projects, again with the appropriate citation. This is complicated by the fact that many electronic resources do not enable this process and further by copyright issues. However, where possible, it should become an option.

Interpretation

The Interpretation stage of the Pathways Model is very important in the information-rich environment of today because students can often locate great quantities of information but this does not become knowledge until they analyze and evaluate it. The Pathways Model provides the following definition of the Interpretation stage:

> *Information requires interpretation to become knowledge. The Interpretation stage engages searchers in the process of analyzing,*

synthesizing and evaluating information to determine its relevancy and usefulness to their research question or information need. Throughout this stage searchers reflect on the information they have gathered and construct personal meaning. (Pappas & Tepe, 1997)

Many of the strategies available in the Interpretation stage represent skills included within other areas of the curriculum. For example students are taught to summarize, paraphrase, and organize information in language arts classes.

Classification, inference, and analysis are skills often used in science. It is important for teachers and LMS to help students apply these as strategies in an information seeking process.

Communication

Students may be able to gather and interpret information to construct their new knowledge, but if they cannot communicate this knowledge they have a problem. The Communication stage is an important part of the Pathways Model, which provides the following definition:

The Communication stage allows searchers to organize, apply, and present new knowledge relevant to their research question or information need. They choose a format that appropriately reflects the new knowledge they need to convey, then plan and create their product. (Pappas & Tepe, 1997)

The most frequent format for students to communicate knowledge is the written paper, which tends to be a textual representation of their research. In this electronic age, the software application of choice may be a word processor, possibly desktop publishing, or a hypertext program, that enables students to integrate text, graphics, photographic images, or video clips. Students may develop mental models that are graphic or image-based rather than text-based. Students must be given opportunities to communicate their new knowledge in the format that best conveys their ideas. This means the end product formats of students' research may differ within the group. This may challenge the teachers' assessment process but enhance student learning.

Evaluation

Evaluation is often seen as the act of a teacher assessing the final product of the students but if students are to become independent learners they must engage in assessing their own process and learn from that experience. The Pathways Model provides the following definition of the Evaluation stage:

Evaluation (self and peer) is ongoing in this nonlinear information process model and should occur throughout each stage. Searchers use their evaluation of the process to make revisions that enable them to develop their own unique information seeking process. It is through this continuous evaluation and revision process that searchers develop the ability to become independent searchers. Searchers also evaluate their product or the results of their communication of new knowledge. (Pappas & Tepe, 1997)

Evaluation must occur throughout every stage of the information seeking process rather than an event that occurs at the end of the project. Searchers need to develop their own information gathering process, a model they can apply every time they need to gather and use information. This process may well be nonlinear; meaning that students will not follow the same pathway through stages of an information seeking process. Each may have a different approach based on individual learning styles, personal preference, or type of project. Students will become aware of this individualized method as they apply their process and engage in self-assessment. The teacher and LMS should facilitate this self-assessment.

Teachers and LMS need strategies to enable an assessment of process. Authentic assessment tools such as logs, journals, conferences, and portfolios are the most useful. Graphic organizers can be developed to help students organize information, log their progress, and provide documentation for teachers and LMS. Students should be encouraged to develop either a paper or electronic trail of their process as well. For example, they might keep citation print outs, or electronic notes in a searching portfolio. Conferencing with students is another way to assess their progress. Conference notes might be kept on students' log sheets. Student-centered learning often

encourages small group projects, which allows some conferencing in those groups. The end product is another means of assessment and students should be encouraged toward both self and peer assessment of the products. If assessment is on going throughout the project, teachers must have a degree of flexibility. An assessment at the Interpretation stage may mean the student needs to return to the Presearch or Search stage. In this type of learning activity, a rigid schedule becomes an inhibiting factor.

Pathways to Knowledge

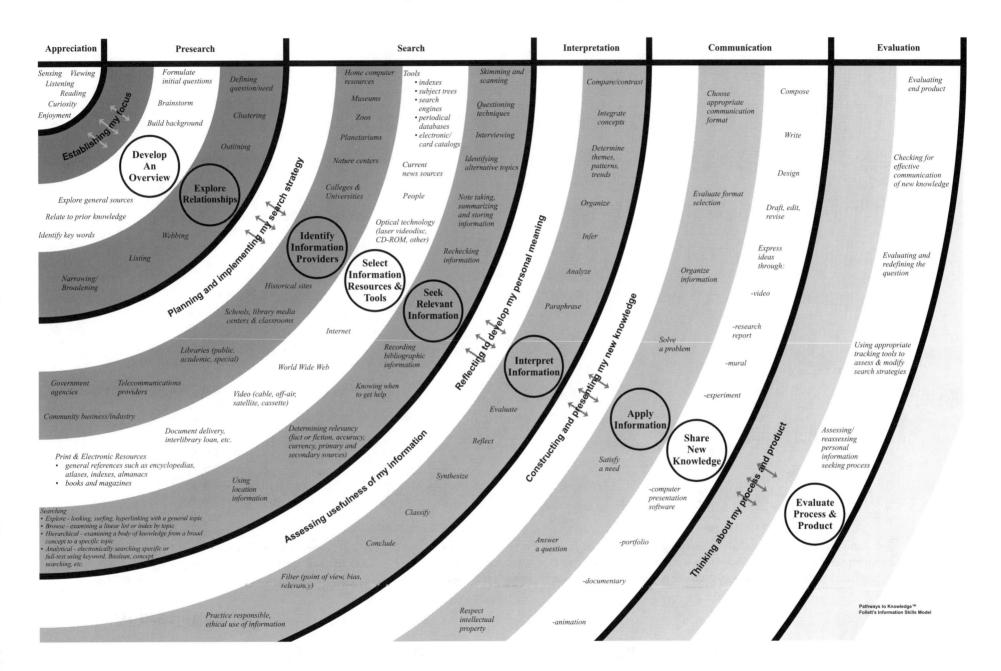

Appreciation

Sensing Viewing
Listening
Reading
Curiosity
Enjoyment

Establishing my focus

Explore general sources

Relate to prior knowledge

Identify key words

Narrowing/
Broadening

Government
agencies

Telecommunications
providers

Community business/industry

Print & Electronic Resources
• general references such as encyclopedias,
  atlases, indexes, almanacs
• books and magazines

Searching
• Explore - looking, surfing, hyperlinking with a general topic
• Browse - examining a linear list or index by topic
• Hierarchical - examining a body of knowledge from a broad
  concept to a specific topic
• Analytical - electronically searching specific or
  full-text using keyword, Boolean, concept
  searching, etc.

Presearch

Formulate
initial questions

Brainstorm

Build background

Defining
question/need

Clustering

Outlining

Develop An Overview

Explore Relationships

Webbing

Listing

Planning and implementing my search strategy

Historical sites

Schools, library media
centers & classrooms

Internet

Libraries (public,
academic, special)

World Wide Web

Video (cable, off-air,
satellite, cassette)

Document delivery,
interlibrary loan, etc.

Using
location
information

Practice responsible,
ethical use of information

Search

Home computer
resources

Museums

Zoos

Planetariums

Nature centers

Colleges &
Universities

Current
news sources

People

Optical technology
(laser videodisc,
CD-ROM, other)

Tools
• indexes
• subject trees
• search
  engines
• periodical
  databases
• electronic/
  card catalogs

Skimming and
scanning

Questioning
techniques

Interviewing

Identifying
alternative topics

Note taking,
summarizing
and storing
information

Rechecking
information

Identify Information Providers

Select Information Resources & Tools

Seek Relevant Information

Recording
bibliographic
information

Knowing when
to get help

Determining relevancy
(fact or fiction, accuracy,
currency, primary and
secondary sources)

Assessing usefulness of my information

Evaluate

Reflect

Synthesize

Classify

Conclude

Filter (point of view, bias,
relevancy)

Respect
intellectual
property

Interpretation

Compare/contrast

Integrate
concepts

Determine
themes,
patterns,
trends

Organize

Infer

Analyze

Paraphrase

Reflecting to develop my personal meaning

Interpret Information

Solve
a problem

Satisfy
a need

Answer
a question

Constructing and presenting my new knowledge

Apply Information

Communication

Choose
appropriate
communication
format

Evaluate format
selection

Organize
information

Compose

Write

Design

Draft, edit,
revise

Express
ideas
through:

-video

-research
report

-mural

-experiment

-computer
presentation
software

-portfolio

-documentary

-animation

Share New Knowledge

Thinking about my process and product

Evaluation

Evaluating
end product

Checking for
effective
communication
of new knowledge

Evaluating and
redefining the
question

Using appropriate
tracking tools to
assess & modify
search strategies

Assessing/
reassessing
personal
information
seeking process

Evaluate Process & Product

Follett's Information Skills Model

Pathways to Knowledge™: Extended Text Version

I. Appreciation

Individuals appreciate literature, the arts, nature and information in the world around them through varied and multiple formats, including stories, film, paintings, natural settings, music, books, periodicals, the Web, video, etc. Appreciation often fosters curiosity and imagination which can be a prelude to a discovery phase in an information seeking activity. As learners proceed through the stages of information seeking their appreciation grows and matures throughout the process.

Strategies include:
© listening
© sensing
© curiosity
© imagining
© viewing
© reading
© creating
© writing
© discussing
© verbalizing
© appreciating
© enjoying
© evaluating

II. Presearch

The Presearch stage enables searchers to make a connection between their topic and prior knowledge. They may begin by brainstorming a web or questions that focus on what they know about their topic and what they want to know. This process may require them to engage in exploratory searching through general sources to develop a broad overview of their topic and explore the relationships among subtopics. Presearch provides searchers with strategies to narrow their focus and develop specific questions or define information needs.

Strategies include:
- © building background information
- © exploring general sources of information
- © relating information to prior knowledge
- © formulating initial questions
- © identifying keywords
- © brainstorming ideas and information about topic
- © relating topics and concepts through webbing, outlining, clustering, etc.
- © narrowing or broadening a topic
- © developing specific research questions
- © defining information needs
- © following procedures for using information technologies and facilities
- © seeking help from appropriate sources when needed
- © evaluating the outcome of Presearch

III. Search

During the Search stage, searchers identify appropriate information providers, resources and tools, then plan and implement a search strategy to find information relevant to their research question or information need. Searchers are open to using print and electronic tools and resources, cooperative searching and interaction with experts.

Strategies include:
© applying resource location skills
© asking questions to clarify meaning
© distinguishing among information sources
© using information sources appropriately
© recording appropriate information through summarizing, quoting
   and listing significant facts (handwritten and/or electronic)
© recording bibliographic information
© gathering information from authentic and human resources
© selecting and using information tools (e.g. indexes, catalogs, bibliographies, directories, search engines)
© developing search strategies for print and electronic resources,
including

Explore Search (looking, surfing, hyperlinking with a general topic)

Browse Search (examining a linear list or index by topic)

Hierarchical Search (examining a body of knowledge from a broad concept to a specific topic)

Analytical Search (electronically searching specified or full text using keyword, Boolean, concept searching, etc.)

   © understanding the concept of linear (print) and nonlinear
      (electronic) organization of information
   © skimming and scanning to gather information
   © determining relevancy of information
      fact or fiction, accuracy, currency, primary and secondary sources, and relevancy to research question or
      information need
   © evaluating the appropriateness of information providers, tools, and resources
   © evaluating the results of the search strategy

IV. Interpretation

Information requires interpretation to become knowledge. The Interpretation stage engages searchers in the process of analyzing, synthesizing and evaluating information to determine its relevancy and usefulness to their research question or information need. Throughout this stage searchers reflect on the information they have gathered and construct personal meaning.

Strategies include:
© inferring
© drawing conclusions
© paraphrasing
© filtering information (point of view, bias, etc.)
© reflecting
© organizing information
© practicing responsible and ethical use of information
© comparing and contrasting
© analyzing
© determining credibility
© classifying
© evaluating information
© understanding cause and effect
© integrating concepts
© synthesizing
© determining themes, patterns, trends
© evaluating information to support or refute a problem, or research question

V. Communication

The Communication stage allows searchers to organize, apply, and present new knowledge relevant to their research question or information need. They choose a format that appropriately reflects the new knowledge they need to convey, then plan and create their product.

Strategies include:
© organizing information
© selecting an appropriate communication format
© applying information to answer a question or solve a problem
© expressing creative ideas through creating, speaking, composing, writing, designing, etc.

© developing a draft or initial version, editing, and revising
© evaluating the format selection
© presenting new knowledge through selected formats
© respecting intellectual property

The communication formats below are a representative sample and are not meant to be an all inclusive list. Some formats are relevant to more than one category and are listed under all that apply. For example, demonstration is listed under both audio and visual. The visual category includes both static and motion visuals. Multimedia is defined as two or more formats. Formats include:

Visual	**Visual/Motion**	**Text**	**Multimedia**
diagram	TV documentary	research paper	sound/slide show
timeline	video tape	writing a book	presentation software
model	animation	book report	exhibit
Venn diagram	video conferencing	crossword puzzle	computer program
slide show	film	journal	portfolio
puppet show		creative writing	Web page
poster		letter writing	
diorama		word find	
transparency	**Oral**	computer program	
art work	panel discussion	newspaper	
graph	music	puzzle	
chart	demonstration	portfolio	
presentation software	travelogue	report	
book jacket	interview	database	
computer program	speech	spreadsheet	
puzzle	debate	story	
display	skit or play	biography	
mural	dialog		
map	story		
graphic			
exhibit			
photograph			
bulletin board			
drawing			
Web page			

VI. Evaluation

Evaluation (self and peer) is ongoing in this nonlinear information process model and should occur throughout each stage. Searchers use their evaluation of the process to make revisions that enable them to develop their own unique information seeking process. It is through this continuous evaluation and revision process that searchers develop the ability to become independent searchers. Searchers also evaluate their product or the results of their communication of new knowledge.

Strategies include:
© evaluating and redefining the question
© assessing/reassessing personal information seeking process
© evaluating end product
© checking for effective communication of new knowledge
© using appropriate tracking tools (e.g. logs, journals) to assess and modify search strategies

Chapter Two: Teaching About Search Strategies

Paper versus Electronic Search Features

Students who want to use electronic information resources, both in CD-ROM format and on the Internet, are faced with a lack of standardization. Books may vary in size and color but most book publishers recognize the importance of a title page, table of contents, page numbers, or an index. Electronic resource publishers have not established basic standards so screen design and search features are typically different in CD-ROM or Internet-based resources. There is some standardization within electronic resources developed by a single publisher. For example, the search features included in the resources published by Gale are the same in *Discovering Authors*, *Discovering Science*, or *Contemporary Authors*. However, there is a great difference in the search features across all the electronic encyclopedias or periodical databases available today.

The standardization of features within paper books has allowed teachers and library media specialists (LMS) to instruct students to recognize these features and develop strategies for accessing information in an efficient and effective manner. For example, most reference and nonfiction paper books have page numbers, chapter headings, a table of contents, and an index. *Use the index*, is an instruction given to students searching for information. Students have learned that an index is organized in alphabetical order, a linear progression, and to find the specific reference they must use the page numbers noted in the index. For example, students looking for information about *China* in an atlas would begin their search by looking in the *C* section of the index. The index indicates the map of China is located on pages 35-36, so they turn to those pages. That is a comfortable, well-used strategy. What happens when these same students look for information in an electronic atlas? Students using the *New Millennium World Atlas Deluxe* (Rand McNally, 1998) see a button labeled *Global Find*. Selection of this button opens a screen with a search box and a list of subjects. Typing *China* in the search box causes the subject list to shift to the *C* section where *China* is located. Double clicking on that subject opens a map of *China*. Do these students understand that this subject list is also an index? Intuitively they probably know that the hyperlinking action of selecting *China*, which opens the map, is the same action as looking for page numbers in the book index. Use of other electronic resources with search features that look for subjects within full text might lead them to think the same action is occurring in *the New Millennium World Atlas Deluxe*, but this is not the case. Analytical, or a full text search feature is not available in this electronic atlas. If students are to be independent users of electronic resources they must have the same understanding of these search features as they do when using paper books. Electronic resources offer search features that are much more sophisticated than those available in paper books and students need to understand how these work, be able to distinguish between them, and know when a specific feature applies to their information need. The challenge to teachers and LMS is teaching students these skills.

Context and Process

Teaching students to use the search features of electronic resources should be developed within the context of a topical instructional activity or unit. Educators today know that skills and knowledge taught within the context of

practical application has the greatest chance of student retention. For example, students learn the basics of graphing but then become more adept at using the skill if their practice occurs during a unit on weather. The same premise applies when teaching students about searching electronic resources. The LMS might instruct students on the four electronic search strategies, Explore, Browse, Hierarchical, and Analytical, (Pappas & Tepe, 1997) followed by a practical application within the context of writing authentic journals on life as a *Native American*.

A focus on process is equally important. The traditional notion of library skills tended to focus on teaching students about specific resources. For example, LMS taught students to use the periodical index, almanacs, or encyclopedias, but the holistic process of gathering, evaluating, and using information was seldom included in this instruction. Students knew how to use specific resources but often lacked the knowledge to be effective information seekers. Process has become a stronger focus across the curriculum today. Educators speak of the writing process or the scientific process. Information seeking must be added to the growing list of process instruction. The Pathways Model

(Pappas & Tepe, 1997) is one example of an information process model. Other process models include, the *Big Six Skills* (Eisenberg and Berkowitz, 1990) or the *Information Literacy Model* (California School Library Association, 1996). [Note: see bibliography for additional models].

Instructional Strategies

Teachers and LMS need to use instructional strategies that encourage students to be independent searchers. One important strategy is the use of graphic organizers that "provide learners with a visual structure that allows them to make connections between topics or concepts, relate to prior knowledge, plan a search strategy, [and] select and evaluate information." (Pappas, 1997) For example, a web is a useful organizer that allows students to identify words and concepts related to their broad research topic. Identifying these keywords is an important first step toward developing a search strategy. Organizers also provide a method of visually arranging information into a useful structure. Some examples of graphic organizers follow at the end of this chapter.

Engaging students in process analysis and evaluation helps them assess which of their strategies were successful and why others were unsuccessful. For example, as students begin a unit on *ecosystems* the LMS might introduce several electronic resources as potential sources of information. She might provide students with a comparison chart, an organizer that would allow students to compare the information retrieved from several sources. As a follow-up, she or the teacher might facilitate small group conferences where students talk about their charts and the usefulness of these resources. This type of sharing discussion might help students assess the process they used to gather information from the resources and the quality of the information gathered in relation to their research question or information need. Evaluation throughout the various stages helps students assess the quality and effectiveness of their information seeking process and this knowledge can be applied to future research projects.

Students need to engage in the same analysis process as they select and apply the four search strategies. Graphic organizers, which allow students to compare the results of various search strategies, provide them with visual evidence of the outcome. For example, students who are working on a project about *Native Americans* might begin by using a

Browse Search in an electronic encyclopedia. The result of that search is one general article about *Native Americans*. An Analytical Search using *Native Americans* identifies 55 hits but these represent all the articles in the encyclopedia where *Native Americans* appeared in the full text. Using a comparison chart as a graphic organizer, the teacher might hold a discussion with students about the outcome of this search. During this comparative discussion students might point out that while the article found through the Browse Search on *Native Americans* was the longest piece of information, it was also very general. Checking out the many references found through their Analytical Search might show them that this type of search provides a broader scope of information. This might be an effective time to demonstrate the use of a Hierarchical Search so students could compare these results with information located through Browse and Analytical Searches.

Search logs or journals are useful strategies to allow students an opportunity to reflect on the results of searches and evaluate their process. For example, logs have great importance for students who are engaged in an Explore Search, which tends to be serendipitous and nonlinear.

Hyperlinking or surfing through an electronic resource can be fun and engage students in exciting discovery activities. However, if the search has a purpose in relation to a proposed project, a log that shows the hyperlink connections provides students with a pathway of their explorations and some documentation if they want to return to sites visited along that pathway. Search logs also encourage students to maintain a record of important resource citations.

The important global instructional strategy for LMS and teachers to remember is that students need opportunities to evaluate their search process so they might make change in their next project and slowly become effective and independent searchers. The evaluative focus is on product and process only within the scope of one project in too many research projects. Yet learning to be an independent searcher is like learning to write, which requires practice, editing and revision over time and many writing experiences. If teachers and LMS apply that global perspective to information seeking, their students will slowly become confident independent searchers.

Figure 1

The Web

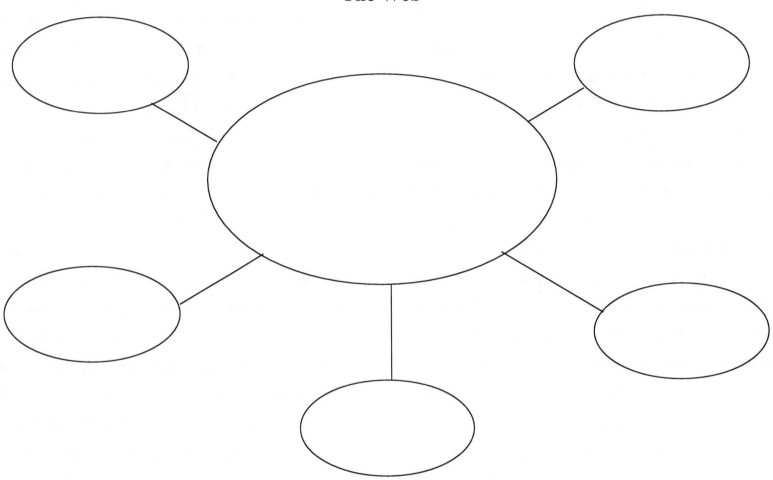

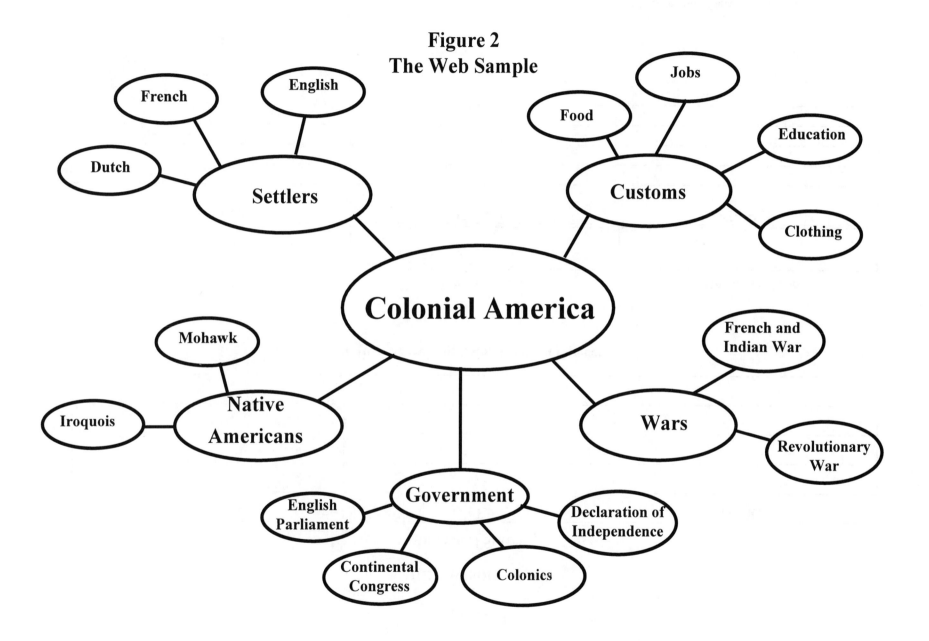

Figure 2
The Web Sample

Colonial America

Settlers
- French
- English
- Dutch

Customs
- Food
- Jobs
- Education
- Clothing

Native Americans
- Mohawk
- Iroquois

Wars
- French and Indian War
- Revolutionary War

Government
- English Parliament
- Continental Congress
- Colonics
- Declaration of Independence

Figure 3

Comparison Chart

Analytical Search

Search Phrase	Hit Rate	Hit Rate

Analytical Searching Using Boolean Operators

Search Phrase	Resource Title	Resource Title
	Hit Rate	Hit Rate

Figure 4

Comparison Chart Sample

Analytical Search

Search Phrase	Resource Title	Resource Title
	Compton's Interactive Encyclopedia 1997	Microsoft Encarta 1997
Search Phrase	**Hit Rate**	**Hit Rate**
Declaration of Independence	2449	495
"Declaration of Independence"	167	4119
"Continental Congress"	122	115
"Native Americans"	180	680

Analytical Searching Using Boolean Operators

Search Phrase	Resource Title	Resource Title
	Compton's Interactive Encyclopedia 1997	Microsoft Encarta 1997
Search Phrase	**Hit Rate**	**Hit Rate**
America **AND** Settlers **AND** Education	19	137
America **AND** Colonies	466	468
America **OR** Colonies	4793	3244
America **NOT** Colonies	3176	1831

Figure 5

Explore Search Log

An Explore Search starts with a topic you are curious about and follows interesting hyperlinks or hot spots. This log lets you keep track of your pathway so you can return to items of special interest. You might use a Web for the same purpose and show how topics are related.

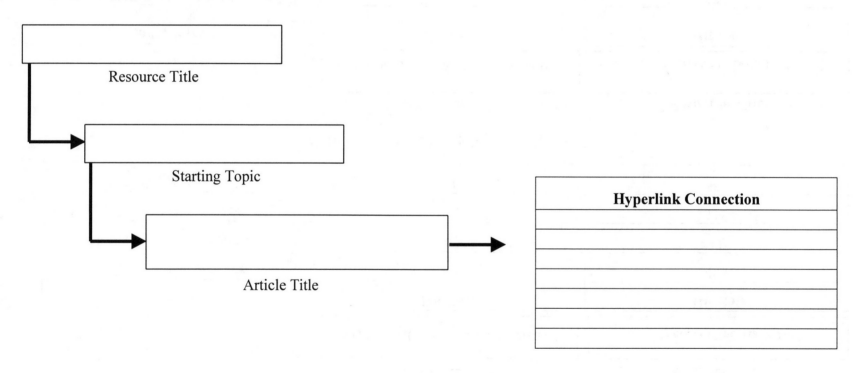

Figure 6

Explore Search Log Sample

An Explore Search starts with a topic you are curious about and follows interesting hyperlinks or hot spots. This log lets you keep track of your pathway so you can return to items of special interest. You might use a Web for the same purpose and show how topics are related.

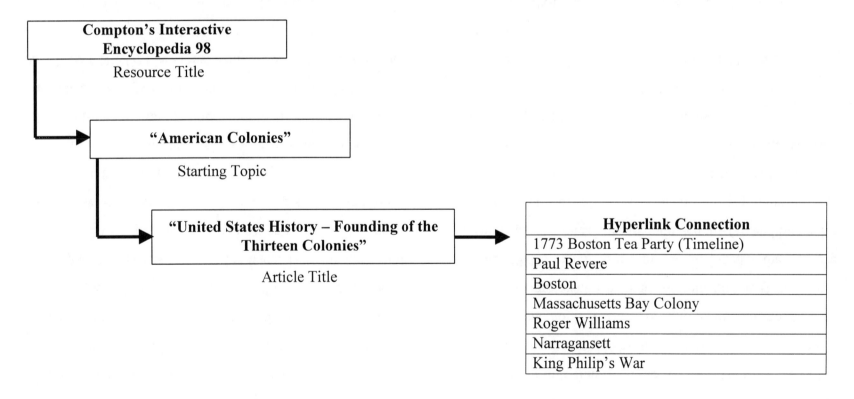

Chapter 3: Changing Search Features of Electronic Resources

The electronic resources included in this book are a representative sample of resources that might typically appear in the reference section of school library media centers. The majority of the titles are general reference resources including encyclopedias, dictionaries, almanacs, and atlases. A sample of periodical databases with full text references and clipping news services has been included. The remainder of the resources have a specific focus and cover a variety of subjects. All were selected using standard reviewing sources and were highly rated by reviewers.

Many of these electronic resources make connections to related information on the Internet or to producers' Web sites for updates. A growing number of resources have both Internet-based and CD-ROM versions. With the exception of *Electric Library* and *Britannica Online*, the book was written based on CD-ROM versions of the resources. The shift from CD-ROM to Internet resources is changing rapidly, but Internet resources often do not include all the multimedia and search features available on the CD-ROM resources. Since the first edition of this book was published, electronic resources now include more media features, e.g. still pictures, motion video, sound clips, etc. Images are available in proximity to the related text by using multiple frames on the screen, allowing the user to view image and text side by side. Many resources provide hypertext and hot link connections to related information.

A significant percentage of both explore (84%) and browse (92%) searching features are included in the resources. Analytical search features are included in 76% and hierarchical search features in only 52%. Some resources produced for younger users tend to include explore features with less emphasis on hierarchical and analytical search features. One criteria applied for the inclusion of a resource was availability of a minimum of two search features. Many resources produced for a younger audience had to be eliminated because the only search feature available was explore.

In all of these electronic resources, the images, video clips, and sound features offer enhancements over print resources that reflect a major shift in information access. The notion that an image can be a powerful message is illustrated in the exciting video clips in the multimedia encyclopedias. For example, watching blood flow through the heart in a motion video clip conveys that information much more clearly than a text description. Images have always been a powerful means of communicating information, but they were difficult to locate. Now many electronic resources allow access to multimedia through captions enabling Explore, Browse, Hierarchical, and Analytical Searches.

Encyclopedias

The electronic encyclopedia is often an early information technology acquisition. To the uninformed they sometimes seem like toys, but they represent a radical shift in the way information is organized and presented. Previously encyclopedias were considered stepping stones to a general understanding of a topic. Students were expected to proceed on to other resources to study the topic in more depth. That premise still applies when a searcher looks up a topic in the index, reads that article or section of an article, and continues the search for that topic in other resources. The difference in an electronic encyclopedia is that when the searcher types a topic in the search box the electronic encyclopedia will list multiple articles that contain that topic. The software looks

through the full text of articles, not just the index, and locates a variety of references that may present the topic in ways totally different from the original concept. Now the searcher can read or view a variety of references, and make hypertext connections to related concepts. This process makes even a general encyclopedia a much more powerful tool in making connections to prior knowledge, building background information, and helping the searcher to examine broader concepts. However, it is important to remember this resource is only an encyclopedia with all the limitations this implies for locating information that requires depth of content knowledge or a specific focus beyond a general perspective.

Dictionaries

Dictionaries are another example of the way a resource changes when the format becomes electronic. Print dictionaries present word definitions and language usage as a static, linear list, always in alphabetical order by the word itself. It is not possible to reorder the list or access the information in any other manner. An electronic dictionary enables a student to easily locate a word even if the correct spelling is flawed. An electronic dictionary can be sorted based on specific parameters. For example, a searcher looking for words of French origin, or perhaps words originated within a specific time period can find them by specifying parameters. Most electronic dictionaries also contain a thesaurus, which can encourage students to broaden their use of language. Some electronic dictionaries include an audio feature that allows users to hear word pronunciation. For example, *The American Heritage Talking Dictionary* presents words in audio.

Atlases

The paper format atlas and gazetteer has been one of the most underused reference resources in the library. Despite the excellent tables and maps using these books was often tedious and students frequently missed information. The electronic atlas and gazetteer offers more efficient access to information through the search engine features. Clicking on a place or geographical feature on a map can connect a searcher to text and multimedia information related to the site. These hypertext connections allow the searcher to access and view images and motion video that represent cultures and countries. The zoom capability of electronic maps allows the searcher to view locations from either a close-up or wide angle perspective. Maps can be redrawn on the screen and printed with graphics, color and parameter options that let students explore relationships and make comparisons. Some atlases include a road map feature that can zoom to a specific address in a city.

Almanacs

In print format the almanac contains much information, but the index is often a weak link to actually finding information. The search engine of the electronic almanac accesses all text, and is not limited to a specific subject vocabulary. Almanacs allow users to print tables and graphics, which makes the information available instantly. The *Time Magazine Multimedia Almanac* is the only full fledged almanac represented in this collection of electronic resources. However, almanacs are included in multiple resource CD-ROMs. For example, *Microsoft Bookshelf* includes *The World Almanac and Book of Facts*.

Periodicals

A periodical database differs from a clipping service. Periodical databases provide subject search and full text access to articles found in magazines. *Readers Guide to*

Periodical Literature, Magazine Article Summaries (MAS), and *ProQuest Direct* are examples of periodical databases. The clipping service is a collection of articles taken from newspapers and other serials, but it does not represent the entire resource. Both periodical and clipping service databases have versions that provide options for bibliographic citation and abstract information as opposed to access to the full text. *SIRS Discoverer*, *SIRS Researcher*, *Newsbank*, and *ProQuest Issue Quest* are examples of clipping services.

Full text is a more expensive option. The search engine is usually the same regardless of the version the library media center may have. Analytical searching, if available, is an important feature in these databases. Explore and hierarchical search features are not typically available in periodical and clipping service databases.

Printing is an important function and many of these databases enable the searcher to create a bibliography from the citations selected. Some of the databases provide the option to select elements of the citation to appear in hard copy while others have a standard format.

Specific Electronic Resources

Electronic resources that focus on a specific subject represent a developing group of CD-ROM resources that are beginning to transform the reference and nonfiction sections of library media centers. In many ways these form a growing collection of exciting electrobooks. The titles included in this book represent high quality resources for various disciplines and levels. Another criteria for inclusion was the availability of search features.

The contrast is great between electronic resources and books on similar topics. Most electronic resources use buttons for hypertext connections, from main menus on an opening screen to graphic screens with icons, which make the nonlinear access to information appear seamless. Information is presented using both text and multimedia, but there is clearly an emphasis on visual and audio formats. Exciting motion video clips convey information beyond that possible in text formats.

Many of these electronic resources would support an interdisciplinary curriculum design because they take a global look at a topical area. David MacCauley's *The Way Things Work* is an excellent example.

Chapter Four
Search Strategy Forms

3D Atlas 98

Publisher: Creative Wonders/ABC Electronic Arts
Date: 1994-97
Grade Level: E -A
Brief Description: An electronic reference that provides different views of our planet through sixteen full-screen Globes. An online connection is available to Maps by Mapquest and Environmental Globe Links.
Printing: Printing of text and pictures is available by selecting File and dragging down to Print.

Format: Macintosh / WIN / MPC CD
Review based on MPC
Help: Help is available on the Menu bar.
Note taking: Select Edit from menu bar and drag down to Copy Postcard Text. This may be pasted to a word processor.

Explore

- Begin exploring by opening one of the pop up screens that changes randomly.
- Continue exploring by selecting Contents from the menu bar. Open any of the menu options listed to see how the CD operates.
- Select Online from the menu bar and explore Maps by Mapquest, Environmental Globe Links, and the 3D Atlas Homepage.

Browse

- To begin a browse search, select Browser from the Contents menu. Click a topic to open more information.
- Continue browsing by using the Find locator, which is available on every screen.
- Find locator allows the searcher to type in a location to search for or highlight a location in the alphabetical listing. Searcher may select Cities, Countries, Country Group, Biomes, Mountains, Ocean Depths, Rivers, Seas and Lakes, or Volcanoes.
- Double click to open article information.

Hierarchical

- Not available.

Analytical

- To begin an analytical search, select Edit from the menu bar and drag down to search.
- This will open a Keyword search. Searcher may type in a keyword. The atlas will locate the keyword within the index and also show all the locations that apply to the keyword.
- Searcher may then highlight the location they would like to view and click the Go To button to open the information.

ABC News Links

Publisher: Creative Wonders/ABC Electronic Arts
Date: 1996
Grade Level: M -S
Brief Description: An electronic reference tool that links current events to historical context. This resource has an online connection to ABC News through *America Online*.
Printing: Printing of text and pictures is available by selecting File and dragging down to Print.

Format: Macintosh / WIN / MPC CD
Review based on Macintosh.
Help: Help is available under the Apple Help Guide.
Note taking: Not available.

Explore

- Begin exploring by selecting Contents from the menu bar. Open any of the menu options listed to see how the CD operates.
- Continue exploring by viewing the Find locator to see all the available areas to search.
- Select WonderLink from the menu bar to Download Latest ABC Update or view the ABC News Archives. This will require a connection to *America Online*.

Browse

- To begin a browse search, select Exhibits Browser from the Contents menu. Click a topic to open more information.
- From the Contents menu select Names and Faces. Select a letter of the alphabet to view pictures and information about famous people.
- Continue browsing by using the Find locator which is available on every screen.
- The Find locator allows the searcher to type in a name of a country to search for or highlight a country name in the alphabetical listing. Searcher may select ABC Regions, Cities, Continents, Countries, Groups. Mountains and Volcanoes, Ocean Depths, Political Systems, Rivers, Seas and Lakes.
- Double click to open article information.

Hierarchical

- Not available.

Analytical

- To begin an analytical search, select Edit from the menu bar and drag down to Search by Keyword.
- This will open a Keyword search. Searcher may type in a keyword. The keyword will be located within the index and will also show all the articles that apply to the keyword.
- Searcher may then highlight the location they would like to view and click the Go To button to open the information.

The American Heritage Talking Dictionary

Publisher: SoftKey Multimedia Inc.
Date: 1995
Grade Level: E -A
Brief Description: Contains the complete *American Heritage Dictionary and Thesaurus and The Dictionary of Cultural Literacy* with audio presentation.
Printing: Printing of text and pictures is available by clicking File on the menu bar and dragging down to Print.

Format: Macintosh/MPC CD
Review based on Macintosh
Help: Help is available under the Apple Menu Guide.
Note taking: Note taking is available by highlighting sections of the text. Click EDIT from menu bar and drag down to Copy. Paste to a word processor.

Explore

- Not available.

Browse

- To begin a browse search, click any word in the Browse Window. Definition will open with pronunciation of the word.
- Select Reference from tool bar and pull down to *The Dictionary of Cultural Literacy* to change alphabetical listing in the Browse Window.
- Click View Button for article information.

Hierarchical

- Not available.

Analytical

- To begin an analytical search, click Tools on the menu bar and pull down to Wordhunter. This opens a search box where the searcher can enter a word to search. Boolean AND/OR/NOT may be used. A search may also be restricted by using subject labels assigned by the publisher. Case sensitive and partial word search may be chosen.
- Word list opens. Double click word to view definition.

Bartlett's Familiar Quotations: Expanded Multimedia Edition

Publisher: Time Warner Electronic Publishing
Date: 1995
Grade Level: M-A
Brief Description: An electronic reference reflecting the works of the sixteenth edition of *Bartlett's Familiar Quotations*. This work adds the multimedia features of videos, sound and still pictures reflecting our language and our culture.
Printing: Not Available.

Format: CD
Review based on: Windows
Help: Available on the Menu Bar.
Note taking: Highlight text and press CTRL +C to copy text to clipboard for pasting in a word processing program.

Explore

- At opening window, click once to open menu screen.
- Explore by selecting from Bartlett's Select Quotations or Media Timeline.
- Essays from the editors and credits are also available buttons.

Browse

- Choose the Bartlett's icon and an alphabetical index of authors opens.
- Browse the author list. To select an author, click once on the name and the quotations attributed to that author will open in the window on the right.
- Author names may also be entered into a search box. Quotations attributed to the author open in the right window.

Hierarchical

- Click on the Select Quotations button.
- Select the New button to open a menu listing for topic, author, date, keyword, source, and media.
- Selecting topic and media opens an hierarchical search menu. Searcher may select combinations of areas to search for quotations.

Analytical

- Click on the Select Quotations button.
- Select the New button to open a menu listing for topic, author, date, keyword, source, and media.

- Select author, date, keyword or source to conduct an analytical search.
- Author searching can be expanded by selecting Category and limiting the search by Gender, Profession, or Region.
- Date searching can be either by a known date or by entering dates in the From and To box.
- Selecting Keyword searching allows the searcher to add any word indexed to their search criteria.
- Source searching lists all the available quoted resources.
  Once the selection criteria are completed, the searcher clicks Find Quotations. Quotations will be selected that match the criteria.

Britannica Online

Publisher: Encyclopaedia Britannica, Inc.
Date: 1997
Grade Level: I–A
Brief Description: This online resource includes all the text of *Encyclopaedia Britannica Print* plus over 3000 additional articles, over 12,000 digital images, over 25,000 Internet links that are tied to the encyclopedia articles, and statistics on over 190 nations. Also includes *Merriam Webster's Collegiate Dictionary, Tenth Edition*.

Printing: Printing is available by selecting File from the menu bar and dragging down to Print, or by selecting the Printer icon on the browser tool bar.
Format: Online
Review based on Online
Help: Help is a button on every screen.
Note taking: Information may be highlighted and copied, then pasted to a word processor.

Explore

- Begin exploring at the main menu screen. Try using the Search, Browse, Site Map and Help buttons that are across the tool bar.
- Scroll down the main menu screen to the special sections Features, Browse A-Z lists, References, and More.
- Continue exploring by entering a word or phrase or question into the search strategy box on the main menu screen. Click search. Look over the result listing to see how articles are presented.

Browse

- To begin a browse search, select the Browse button from the main menu screen. This opens a basic search strategy box. The searcher may enter a search term Click Search
- A results listing will open and the searcher may select to view the listing by Articles, Index, Dictionary, Illustrated Articles, Illustrations, Knowledge in Depth, Yearbooks, Geography, Biographies, Internet Links, and Multimedia. The searcher may also decide to display Titles Only.
- Click article link to open article. How to cite the article in a bibliography is listed at the bottom of the article.
- The Topic Map that opens with the article allows the searcher to know what is open on the screen.

Hierarchical

- To begin an hierarchical search, select Spectrum from the main menu. This gives the searcher a categorical listing.
- The searcher may select any category and continue to link through the subcategories until an article opens.

Analytical

- To begin an analytical search, select Search from the tool bar. The searcher has the option of searching in Natural Language format or using Boolean logic.
- The searcher may enter their word, phrase or question into the Standard Search format. The searcher must select either article, index or dictionary to search within.
- If Boolean logic is utilized in the search, remember to use ALL CAPITAL LETTERS for AND, OR, AND NOT, and ADJ.
- If Enhanced Search is chosen, the searcher must decide how to display, sort and list.
- Click the Search button. A results listing will open. Click on any of the linked articles. Internet Links are shown also.
- Click the article link to open the article.

Cartopedia: The Ultimate World Reference Atlas

Publisher: Dorling Kindersley Multimedia
Date: 1995
Grade Level: E -A
Brief Description: An electronic world reference atlas listing 193 country articles.
Printing: Printing of text and pictures is available by clicking the Options button on the Navigation Panel. Select Print.

Format: Macintosh / MPC CD
Review based on Macintosh
Help: Help is available on the Navigation Panel by clicking the Question Mark.
Note taking: Not available

Explore

- Begin exploring by allowing the CD to open to the spinning globe.
- Select from The Political World, The Physical World, A to Z Countries, Index, or World View to begin further exploration.

Browse

- To begin a browse search, select A to Z countries.
- Choose the letter of the alphabet of the country to view.
- Country names within that letter are listed. Double click on a country to open a synopsis of the country and the Navigation Panel with additional buttons for more statistical information about the country.

Hierarchical

- To begin an hierarchical search, select Index on the Navigation Panel.
- The Index box opens allowing the searcher to select from General, People, Physical Features and Places.
- Selecting any of these areas will open an alphabetical index listing places by their native language pronunciation and their English equivalent.
- Highlight a selection and click OK.
- The place selected will open with additional statistical information options available on the Navigation Panel.

Analytical

- Not available.

Collier's Encyclopedia 1998

Publisher: Sierra On-line, Inc.
Date: 1998
Grade Level: M-A
Brief Description: This multimedia encyclopedia includes an atlas, timeline, and the American Heritage Dictionary. Links to many resources on the Web.
Printing: Select Print icon from the top Menu Bar. Cursor must be positioned within the frame to be printed.

Format: CD
Review based on: Windows
Help: Select Question mark [?] from icons on side Menu Bar.
Note taking: Use Netscape Communicator's Composer as a word processor for notes.

Explore	Browse	Hierarchical	Analytical
• Click on Atlas icon located on side Menu Bar. Click place names on maps to hyperlink to articles and multimedia.	• Click on the Encyclopedia icon in the side Menu Bar.	• Click on the Encyclopedia icon in the side Menu Bar.	• Click on the Encyclopedia icon in the side Menu Bar.
• Click on Timeline icon located on side Menu Bar. Type year in box select from decade list. Click on hot spots to make hyperlink connections to articles.	• Select Encyclopedia Index A-Z under Explore and click to open.	• Select Topic Finder under Explore and click to open.	• For a Simple Search, type word or phrase in Search Box and press Enter.
• Encyclopedia articles include See Also hot spots that hyperlink to other articles.	• Click on the volume letter that represents the search word.	• Click on the broad topic that best represents the search word.	• For a Complex Search, use Boolean operators AND, OR, NOT to combine multiple words or phrases.
	• On the next screen, click on the double letters that represent the first two letters of the search word.	• Select article and click to open; or	• For a Concept Search, enter a question beginning with Who, What, Where, When.
	• When search word appears in article title list, click to open.	• Select category and continue to make category selections until appropriate article appears.	• Articles are listed in the order or relevancy to search word. Click on title or subject in results list to open article.
		• To back up click on the last blue topic in the Topics List.	

Compton's Interactive Encyclopedia, 1998 Edition

Publisher: The Learning Company
Date: 1997
Grade Level: E-S
Brief Description: Contains the complete 26-volume encyclopedia, an atlas, dictionary/thesaurus, planetarium, timeline, pictures, motion video, audio clips, and direct Web links.
Printing: Select the Print button from the Menu Bar.

Format: CD
Review based on: Windows
Online Help: Help is located on the menu bar
Online Note taking: Highlight text to copy, select Notepad or Word Processor from the Tools menu on the Menu Bar. A specific Word Processor can be selected by opening Preferences under the Help button.

Explore

- Begin exploring by selecting Explore, Planetarium, Recent Events, and Exploring Questions from the Special menu on the Menu Bar.
- Or, searchers may explore by selecting the Timeline or Atlas buttons on the Menu Bar.
- Searchers may explore by double clicking on hyperlink text or pictures that connect to articles in Comptons or with URLs to the Web.

Browse

- To begin a browse search, select List of Contents A-Z from the Find menu on the Menu Bar.
- Type partial word or word in search box; title list moves to appropriate section of alphabetical listing..
- Select desired article and double click to open.
- To narrow the browse search, change the Look For list from All Contents to a specific medium, for example, articles, videos, etc.

Hierarchical

- To begin an hierarchical search, select Topic Tree from the Find menu on the Menu Bar.
- The Topic Tree list opens. Double click on a topic to open branching subtopic lists.
- Enlarging Topic Tree to full screen (clicking on button in upper right corner of title bar) enables searcher to view branching lists.
- Continue to double click on topics until title list appears.
- Double click on title to open article, picture, video, etc.
- Clicking on previous topic lists enables searcher to redirect the search or begin again.

Analytical

- To begin an analytical search, select Word Search from the Find menu on the Menu Bar.
- For a simple search, enter a word or phrase in the search dialog box. Click the Search button. A selection list opens. Highlight topic of interest and double click to open.
- For a complex search, select the More Options button. Use the additional search boxes and Boolean operators (and, or, not) to broaden or narrow the search. Filters that appear on this screen enable the searcher to specify the type of information to be searched (e.g. text, pictures, video, audio).

Contemporary Authors on CD

Publisher: Gale
Date: 1997
Grade Level: E-A
Brief Description: Contains biographical and bibliographical information on current important authors and includes full text of complete print version.
Printing: Available under File on Menu Bar.

Format: CD
Review based on: Windows
Help: Available on Menu Bar
Note taking: Not available

Explore
- Not available

Browse
- Select Search from Menu Bar.
- Pull down menu options Author, Title, Nationality/Ethnicity, and Literary Genre all contain browse search features through an index.
- Select one option, for example, Author. All four search options follow the same procedure.
- Author Search window opens.
- Enter name in Search Box.
- Click on Count button to see number of entries with specified name. Click on Search button to see Results list. Double

click to open author article.
- Click on New Search or Change Search buttons to start over or revise the search.

Hierarchical
- Not available.

Analytical
- Select Search from Menu Bar.
- Pull down menu options Personal Data and Advanced Search contain analytical search features.
- Selecting Personal Search opens Personal Data Search window with 3 tabs [Author Profile, Personal Facts, and Professional Facts]. This feature searches full text in the Personal Data field only.
- Type words in Search Boxes where appropriate. Filling more boxes narrows the search. Click on the category buttons [Ex: Birth date] to view an index list for each category. Click on the Select Item button to add index words to Search Box.

- Multiple words can be joined with Boolean operators [and, or, not] within each category.
- Click on Count button for number of hits. Click on Search button for Results list. Double click on name to open article.
- To search all text, select Search on the Menu Bar and select Advance Search which opens window.
- Type words and/or phrases in Search Box connected by Boolean operators [and, or, not, near]. Put phrases in quotation marks.
- Click on the Count button to view number of hits. Click on Search button to view results list. Double click on name to open article.

Current Biography 1940-Present

Publisher: H.W. Wilson
Date: 1997
Grade Level: J-A
Brief Description: An electronic reference for more than 15,000 biographies of people of the 20th century.
Printing: Select the Print button at bottom of each citation.

Format: Macintosh / MPC CD
Review based on Macintosh
Help: Help is available on the menu bar and within each citation.
Note taking: Notetaking is available through the Save feature within each citation.

Explore
- Not available.

Browse
- With the WilsonDiscs CD Rom Retrieval System, Browse is an immediate choice at the opening screen.
- Click the Browse button to open the alphabetical listing of search terms.
- Click in the search box, type in the search term and click Browse. Search term will be highlighted with the number of citations in an alphabetical listing. Select Display and citation with available text will open. Select List from Citation Box tool bar for a complete list of Citations.
- To refine a Browse search, click the Category button to select Subjects, All Terms, Topics, Names, Professions.

Type in a search term and select Browse.

Hierarchical
- Not available.

Analytical
- To begin an analytical search, click Keyword Search from the opening screen or select Window on the menu bar and drag down to Search: Keyword.
- The searcher has the option of entering a Name, Profession, Keyword and selecting And or And Not. Selecting Options on the tool bar allows additional search terms, such as Place of Origin, Date of Birth, Race and Ethnicity, Gender.
- Click Search and the first Citation will open. A citation listing is available by clicking on List located on the tool bar.

DISCovering U.S. History

Publisher: Gale Research, Inc.
Date: 1997
Grade Level: M- A
Brief Description: An electronic resource for thousands of essays dealing with historical periods, people, political and cultural events in United States history. Features *Merriam Webster's Biographical Dictionary* and *Merriam Webster's Collegiate Dictionary, Tenth Edition*.
Printing: Printing is available under Options button on opening screen or as a Printer icon on tool bar of an open document.

Format: Win / MPC CD
Review based on MPC
Help: Help is available as a button on each screen.
Note taking: Select Disk icon on the tool bar of an open document to save the document for further use.

Explore

- Begin exploring at the opening screen by selecting Timeline, Search by Name, Search by Subject, Search by Place, Primary Documents, or Picture Gallery buttons. This will allow the searcher to view the various items available on this CD.
- Selecting any of these will open lists which can be explored further by double clicking to open a document

Browse

- To begin a browse search, type in a word or phrase on the search bar of the opening screen. This will open a results list and the first document in the list.
- Searcher may also select Timeline, Search by Name, Search by Subject, Search by Place, or Primary Documents. Topics to open will be highlighted within the listing. Click Select to open document information. Document opens on right and results list will open on left.

Hierarchical

- Searcher may select Search by Subject from main menu screen.
- Instead of choosing the default alphabetical listing, the searcher should click the Outline button. Category folders appear.
- Double click a category name to view subcategories. Select a subcategory to open the information.

Analytical

- To begin an analytical search, select the Full Text Search button.
- This will open a search box. Enter word(s) or phrases (in quotation marks) that should be searched. This will open documents containing the search request.

- Selecting Custom Search from the main menu offers another analytical search.
- Type the search term next to the category (full text, name, occupation, gender, birth date, death date, places, important dates, nationality, or subject) or click on the category name to generate a list of search terms.
- Next select where to search. Clicking the Select All button will select all places to search.
- Select View Documents to get a list of all documents that match the search criteria. Click on entry to display it.

DISCovering World History

Publisher: Gale Research, Inc.
Date: 1997
Grade Level: M- A
Brief Description: An electronic resource for thousands of essays dealing with historical periods, people, political and cultural world events. Features *Merriam Webster's Biographical Dictionary* and *Merriam Webster's Collegiate Dictionary, Tenth Edition*.
Printing: Printing is available under Options button on opening screen or as a Printer icon on tool bar of an open document.

Format: Win / MPC CD
Review based on MPC
Help: Help is available as a button on each screen.
Note taking: Select Disk icon on the tool bar of an open document to save the document for further use.

Explore

- Begin exploring at the opening screen by selecting Timeline, Search by Name, Search by Subject, Search by Place, Primary Documents, or Picture Gallery buttons. This will allow the searcher to view the various items available on this CD.
- Selecting any of these will open lists which can be explored further by double clicking to open a document.

Browse

- To begin a browse search, type in a word or phrase on the search bar of the opening screen. This will open a results list and the first document in the list.
- Searcher may also select Timeline, Search by Name, Search by Subject, Search by Place, or Primary Documents. Topics to open will be highlighted within the listing. Click Select to open document information. Document opens on right and results list will open on left.

Hierarchical

- Searcher may select Search by Subject from main menu screen.
- Instead of choosing the default alphabetical listing, the searcher should click the Outline button. Category folders appear.
- Double click a category name to view subcategories. Select a subcategory to open the information.

Analytical

- To begin an analytical search, select the Full Text Search button.
- This will open a search box. Enter word(s) or phrases (in quotation marks) that should be searched. This will open documents containing the search request.

- Selecting Custom Search from the main menu offers another analytical search.
- Type the search term next to the category (full text, name, occupation, gender, birth date, death date, places, important dates, nationality, or subject) or click on the category name to generate a list of search terms.
- Next select where to search. Clicking the Select All button will select all places to search.
- Select View Documents to get a list of all documents that match the search criteria. Click on entry to display it.

Electric Library

Publisher: Infonautics Corporation
Date: 1997
Grade Level: I -A
Brief Description: Online access to 150 full-text newspapers, hundreds of full-text magazines, two international newswires, two thousand classic books, and thousands of photos.
Printing: Printing is available by selecting File from the menu bar and dragging down to Print, or by selecting the Printer icon on the browser tool bar.

Format: Online
Review based on Online
Help: Help is a button on the main screen.
Note taking: Information may be highlighted and copied, then pasted to a word processor.

Explore
- Begin exploring by selecting About, Help, Contact Us, Feedback, or What's New buttons.
- Continue exploring by looking over the various search strategies available. For example, look at the links to Boolean Search, Natural Language Search, Search Options, View Sources, Search Help and Classic Site.
- Classic Site is a link for those searchers who need to use *Netscape 2.x* or *MSIE 2.x* or lower browsers.

Browse
- To begin a browse search, enter a question or a keyword into the search strategy box that is open on the main screen.
- For a browse search, the searcher should decide to search within Magazines, Books, Newspapers, Pictures, Maps, and TV and Radio Transcripts. Click the Search button.
- The results listing will open. The searcher may view either a detailed list or a list by relevancy, date, size or reading level. All articles listed show what type of source they are from.
- The searcher has the option to Refine Search or Start New Search.

- Click the linked article to open it. On the open document screen, the searcher may select the Go To Best Part button to view the most pertinent article information.

Hierarchical
- Not available.

Analytical
- To begin an analytical search, select Search Options from the main screen. The searcher may either select Natural Language or Boolean Search.
- If the searcher selects Natural Language and then enters a topic, they may limit the search by publication range or search by bibliographic information. The searcher must also select what type of sources.

(magazine, newspaper, etc.) to search within. The searcher may also decide how many results should be listed.
- Click search and the results listing will open. To open the full text of an article, click any article link.
- If the searcher selects a Boolean Search, a search strategy box opens allowing the searcher to select from And, Or, And Not along with selecting the sources to search within, the publication dates, and bibliographic information. The searcher may also decide how many results should be listed.
- Click search and results listing will open. To open the full text of an article, click any article link.

Earth Quest

Publisher: DK Multimedia
Date: 1997
Grade Level: J-A
Brief Description: Uses games and multimedia to present information on earth science. Links to DK Web site.
Printing: Available from the Options menu on the red eye icon.

Format: CD
Review based on: Windows
Help: Available on red eye icon.
Note taking: Not available.

Explore
- Four main rooms [Violent Earth, Mining, Earth Gallery, and Shaping the Earth] lead to games, activities, and information.
- Buttons, icons, and text hyperlink to pictures, videos, and text.

Browse
- Select Index from the red eye icon.
- Click on main index or video index to select.
- Type word or phrase in Search Box.
- Select article and click on the OK button.
- Article or glossary entry opens.

Hierarchical
- Not available.

Analytical
- Not available.

Encyclopedia Americana on CD-ROM

Publisher: Grolier Educational
Date: 1997
Grade Level: M -A
Brief Description: An electronic reference bookshelf containing the contents of the 30-volume printed version of the *Encyclopedia Americana* along with *Merriam-Webster's Collegiate Dictionary Tenth Edition,* Helicon Publishing Company's *Chronology of World History,* and the Academic Press *Dictionary of Science & Technology.* Access to selected World Wide Web sites is through the Grolier Internet Index.

Printing: Printing of text and pictures is available by clicking on the Print button from the tool bar.
Format: Macintosh /Win/ MPC CD
Review based on Macintosh
Help: Help is available from the Help Desk on the tool bar.
Note taking: Note taking is available by clicking on the Notes button on the tool bar. The searcher may take online notes and save them.

Explore

- Begin exploring by opening the various books available for searching. See what type of information will be available from the various books on the bookshelf.
- Explore how *Encyclopedia Americana* utilizes the World Wide Web feature. Click on the WWW button when it appears in an article. If there is Internet access, the searcher will be connected to a web browser and sites relating to the topic searched will be listed.

Browse

- To begin a browse search, select an index to search. Choices are Article Titles, Full Text, Bibliography, Subject , Contributor, Geography, Article Form, User Notes, Maps.
- Type a search request in the search box after selecting an index. The search term will be located within the alphabetical listing. Double click to open the article.

Hierarchical

- To begin an hierarchical search, the searcher should select Article Form from the Index guide for the *Encyclopedia Americana* to get an hierarchical search index.
- Selecting a subject area, the searcher may then double click to view subtopics. Continuing to double click through subtopic choices will open an article.
- Using *The Chronology of World History* or *The Dictionary of Science & Technology*, the searcher can also open hierarchical listings by selecting the type of index.

Analytical

- For an advanced search, click the Advanced Search button on the tool bar. A search window will open allowing the searcher to select a Global Search or Detailed Search.
- A Global Search will look in all the books selected by a searcher. Boolean AND/OR/NOT may be used as well as selecting index type. The number of matches are shown and clicking on the Results button shows the complete search result list.
- A Detailed Search will search multiple indexes within one book at a time. This search strategy also utilizes Boolean operators.

Encyclopedia of Careers and Vocational Guidance

Publisher: J.G. Ferguson Publishing Company
Date: 1997
Grade Level: M - A
Brief Description: An electronic encyclopedia of careers listing 68 industry profiles, 521 job articles, photographs, disability, apprenticeship, and internship indices.
Printing: Printing available by clicking File on the menu bar and dragging down to Print.

Format: Macintosh /Win/ MPC CD
Review based on Macintosh
Help: Help is available on the menu bar.
Note taking: Searcher may make annotations by selecting Book from the menu bar and clicking on Annotations. Types of annotations available are creating a Hyperlink, opening a Bookmark, or starting a Note.

Explore
- Begin exploring by reviewing items listed in the Table of Contents.
- Take time to view the Welcome, How to Use and Graphs section of the Main Menu.

Browse
- To begin a browse search, click the + sign by Job Title Index. The alphabet opens and the searcher may click on the + sign by the letter to view the jobs listed.
- Once a title has been selected, double click on the title to view the pertinent information.
- Follow the same process for all items listed in theTable of Contents.

Hierarchical
- A form of hierarchical searching is available by selecting a specific career or job title. Clicking on that career classification system or job title will list the related occupational subheadings.
- Double click on any information topic and more information will open in the right hand column.

Analytical
- To begin an analytical search, select Book from the tool bar and click on Fielded Search.
- Fielded search allows the searcher to select from boxes such as Personal Interest, School Subject, Salary, Work Environment, etc. The searcher may also enter a job title with AND/OR options. Click the Search button to view results.
- A search results box will open where the searcher may double click an occupation to open it for more information.
- A find box is also available to search for words within the full text.

Exegy

Publisher: ABC-Clio
Date: 1994-1996
Grade Level: M- A
Brief Description: Subscription source for current world information, current events, maps, documents, world facts and figures, biographies and sports.
Printing: Printing of text and pictures is available by clicking the Printer icon on tool bar.

Format: Macintosh / MPC CD
Review based on Macintosh
Help: Help (?) is available on the tool bar.
Note taking: Note taking is available by highlighting sections of the text. Select the Copy button from the tool bar. Next, click the Word Processor button on the tool bar. Exegy will open a selected word processor. Use the Paste function within the word processor to paste the copied text. Return to Exegy.

Explore	Browse	Hierarchical	Analytical
• Begin exploring by clicking the World button on the opening screen. • The Contents screen opens with selections for Countries, International, Sports, Maps. Select one to continue exploring. • Hyperlinks (color highlighted word) within each article links searcher to the glossary or other articles.	• To begin a browse search, select either Countries, International, Sports, or Maps from the Contents menu. • For example, clicking the Countries buttons opens an alphabetical listing of countries. Click on a country to open the article.	• No specific hierarchical search. However, within each article there is a hierarchical category menu. Clicking on this menu opens additional categories related to the article. The hierarchy of the article is tracked below the menu bar.	• To begin a simple analytical search, click the Index button on the tool bar. • The Index opens an alphabetical list. Selecting Keyword group at the bottom of the Index list allows the searcher to choose which Keyword group to view alphabetically. • Next, highlight alphabetical topic to search. Double click to open topic information.

Eyewitness Encyclopedia of Nature

Publisher: DK Multimedia
Date: 1997
Grade Level: E-J
Brief Description: A multimedia compendium with an emphasis on hyperlink connections to information on the natural world. Links to DK Web site.
Printing: Available from the Options menu, a button on the left edge of the screen.

Format: CD
Review based on: Windows
Help: Available from the Options menu.
Note taking: Not available

Explore

- The start up screen is a collection of unusual objects each with a button that hyperlinks to other pictures and text.
- Included on the Start up screen are buttons to Habitats, Prehistoric Life, Animal Vision, Ecology, Bird Calls, The Macro World, Fish, Mammals, Amazing Close-ups, and Classification.
- Clicking each of these buttons opens screens that present information as images and text.
- Articles and pictures include text and hotspots that link to other information.

Browse

- For an index of topics, select the A-Z button on the right edge of start-up screen.
- Enter word in Search Box and press Enter.
- Selecting the Movie Index, Animation, or Animals Sounds buttons allows the searcher to view a list of titles by specific media types.

Hierarchical

- Clicking on Navigator button on the top left edge of the Start up screen opens a hierarchical screen with 15 broad topics in the left column.
- Selection of a topic opens another list with more specific topics.
- Continue topic selection in this manner until the final list opens. Select a specific topic and click to open.

Analytical

- Not available.

Eyewitness History of the World

Publisher: Dorling Kindersley Multimedia
Date: 1995
Grade Level: J-S
Brief Description: Multimedia reference guide to world history.
Printing: Printing of text and pictures is available by clicking the Options button on the Travel Console and select Print.

Format: Macintosh / MPC CD
Review based on Macintosh
Help: Help button (?) is available on Travel Console.
Note taking: Options button on Travel Console has Copy available.

Explore

- Begin exploring by clicking on the various parts of the Travel Console to see what each button opens.

Browse

- To begin a browse search, click on the A-Z Index button on the right hand side of the Travel Console.
- Searchers have the option to select from Main Index or Video Index. Searchers may type in a word to search or select from the alphabetical list. Click the OK button and the selection will open. To begin a browse search, select Who's Who from the Travel Console.
- The searcher may also select Who's Who from the Travel Console. Selecting this book, the searcher then has the option to open a tabbed index of pages of an alphabetical listing of historically famous people.
- The See Also button leads the searcher to additional topics of related information.

Hierarchical

- To begin an hierarchical search, select books from the Travel Console that lead to the historical themes of Culture, Everyday Life, Innovations.
- Selecting a book, the searcher then has the option to open a tabbed index of pages of subtopics related to the area selected. An example would be selecting Innovations. The subtopics would be Inventions, Transportation and Weapons.

Analytical

- Not available.

Find It! Science

Publisher: Follett Software Co.
Date: 1996
Grade Level: E - S
Brief Description: Find It! Science is an electronic guide to selecting quality science literature.
Printing: A Printer button is available within each book information screen.

Format: Macintosh
Review based on Macintosh
Help: Help is available on the tool bar.
Note taking: Not available.

Explore

- Begin exploring by selecting any of the items available on the opening screen. Click on Author, Titles and Series, Keywords, Subjects, What Kind?, Special Requests, or Brainstorms to see ideas to explore.

Browse

- To begin a browse search, select an area from the opening screen, such as Brainstorms.
- Select a specific Brainstorm and then begin to limit the search by choosing Subject, Kind, Special or Wonders from the tool bar. Each addition to the search will register in the Find It! List. Searchers may open book selections by using the Click Here for Books button.

Hierarchical

- To begin an hierarchical search, select Subjects, What Kind?, Special Requests, or Brainstorms from the opening screen.
- Selecting any of these allows the searcher to open subheadings. Search strategy can be seen under Find It! List and Books can be opened by using the Click Here for Books button.

Analytical

- To begin a simple analytical search, select either Author, Titles and Series, or Keywords from the opening screen.
- An index screen will open that can be scrolled through, or a search box is available to type in a search term. Click search selection or Add to List button. Search term will be added to Find It! List of search criteria. Continue to build the search list until the number of books to search is narrowed.

The Grolier Multimedia Encyclopedia 1998-2-CD Deluxe Edition

Publisher: Grolier Interactive, Inc.
Date: 1997
Grade Level: E - A
Brief Description: A two CD electronic encyclopedia with hypertext links to *Encyclopedia Americana* and *The New Book of Knowledge* and with web links through the Online Knowledge Explorer to the *Grolier Internet Index*. Also includes *The American Heritage College Dictionary, Third Edition*.
Printing: Printing of text and pictures is available by clicking Print on the tool bar.

Format: Macintosh / MPC CD
Review based on Macintosh
Help: Help is available on the menu bar and also on the startup screen.
Note taking: Note taking is available by highlighting sections of the text. Click Copy from tool bar. Click Tools on menu bar and drag down to Word Processor. Linked word processor will open. Go to Edit on menu bar, drag down to Paste.

Explore

- Begin exploring at opening screen by selecting either Guided Tour, Navigation/Help or Start.
- Continue exploring at the main screen by selecting Gallery, Timelines, Atlas, or Interactivities.
- Explore the Dictionary and Online button connected to an opened article.

Browse

- To begin a browse search, select Start from Main Menu.
- Searcher may click Browse tab and Articles, Gallery, Atlas, or Timelines to open an alphabetical listing of possible resources. .
- Searcher may type a topic into the search box. Topic will be highlighted within the alphabetical listing. Double click highlighted topic to open the article.
- Selecting the History button lists all items the searcher has visited.
- Use the Online Knowledge Explorer to view additional article information available from *Encyclopedia American, The New Book of Knowledge* or *Grolier Internet Index*.

Hierarchical

- Hierarchical searching is combined with browse searching. When browse searching is selected, the searcher has the choice to select All or Custom. If Custom is selected, searchers may then click Filter to select specific categories and sub-categories to include in an hierarchical search. The list of information changes to show the filtered choices. Double click entries to open articles.

Analytical

- To begin an analytical search, click Search tab and enter a simple search topic. A listing of articles, media and pictures will open.

- Highlight choice and double click to open.
- If the searcher wishes to conduct a more specific search, select Search and Complex. A tiered search strategy box will open. Boolean search terms, Scope for limiters, Media Type and Category are available to help the searcher. Click the Search button and a listing of topic choices will open. Highlight choice and double click to open.
- Use the Online Knowledge Explorer to view additional article information available from *Encyclopedia American, The New Book of Knowledge* or *Grolier Internet Index*.

Interactive Science Encyclopedia

Publisher: Steck-Vaughn Co.
Date: 1997
Grade Level: I- S
Brief Description: An electronic science encyclopedia containing articles, interactive experiments, charts, pictures, videos, animations and sound.
Printing: Select the Print button on the tool bar.

Format: Macintosh / MPC CD
Review based on MPC
Help: Help is available on the tool bar.
Note taking: Select the Notes button on the tool bar to take notes.

Explore

- Begin exploring by reading the Fun Facts box. Pick Next Fact button to see more facts or the Article button to read more information.
- Continue exploring by selecting the Timeline, Labtime, Articles, Topics, or Search buttons.

Browse

- To begin a browse search, select the Articles button from the Main Menu screen.
- Select the Browse tab and then A to Z articles to view an alphabetical listing. Select All Media or specific media.
- Browse searching may be continued by selecting Labtime, Topics or Timeline from the A-Z selection menu.
- Once the alphabetical list appears, highlight the desired topic and double click to open the article.

Hierarchical

- To begin an hierarchical search, select Topics from the Main Menu or the Article Screen.
- Select a topic and double click to open the articles of the subtopics.

Analytical

- To begin an analytical search, select search from the Main Menu.
- The search screen opens. The searcher is given the option of Natural Language searching, Word/Phrase searching, or Complex searching.
- Selecting Natural Language allows the searcher to type in a science question. A list of suggested articles will open.

- Word or phrase searching is also a choice. Truncation using an asterisk may be used.
- Selecting Complex searching, allows the searcher to use Boolean operators. Type in a search term and select from And/Or/Not/Near.
- Article choices will open. Select an article and click the Go To button to open it.

Landmark Documents in American History

Publisher: Facts on File, Inc.
Date: 1995
Grade Level: M- A
Brief Description: An electronic resource for more than 1,200 key documents in American history.
Printing: Printing is available under the Tools button on the screen of an open document.

Format: Win / MPC CD
Review based on MPC
Help: Help is available as a button on each screen.
Note taking: Select Tools button on the screen of an open document. Click Save to save document to disk for further use.

Explore

- Begin exploring at opening screen by selecting Document Title, Subject, Historical Time Period, Year, or People buttons.
- Selecting any of these will open lists which can be explored further by double clicking to open a document.
- Within the open document, explore the Further Readings, About This Document, Biographies or Graphics button.

Browse

- To begin a browse search, select Document Title, Subject, Historical Time Period, Year, or People buttons..
- Selecting any of these will open an alphabetical or numerical list. A search box is available to enter a document title, name, or date. Search topic will be highlighted within the listing. Click Select to open document information. Select Results List button to return to listing of search results.

Hierarchical

- Not available.

Analytical

- To begin an analytical search, click Advanced Search from the opening screen. A search dialog box will open.
- Searcher may enter search terms by Keyword, Subject, Period, Document Type, People, or Country and also by entering dates to search by. If help is needed to decide a term to use, the searcher may click the Keyword, Subject, Period, Document Type, People, or Country button to select terms from a listing. Click Paste button to paste term selected into search box.
- Use Search button to start search. A results list will open. The searcher may highlight document to open and select View Document to open the requested information.

Magazine Articles Summaries FullTEXT Premier

Publisher: Ebsco Publishing
Date: 1997
Grade Level: M- A
Brief Description: Periodical database indexing and abstracting hundreds of thousands of magazine article summaries along with full text articles.
Printing: Printing available by clicking on File on the menu bar, drag down to Print. Searcher may also select Print Marked Items from the File menu. Any items marked in the results list will be printed.

Format: Macintosh / MPC CD
Review based on Macintosh
Online Help: Help is available on the menu bar.
Online Note taking: Note taking is available by selecting Edit from the menu bar and dragging down to Copy to File, Copy Marked Items to File or Copy Selection to File.

Explore
- Not available.

Hierarchical
- Not available.

Browse
- To begin a browse search, select database to search. Press enter.
- Select Windows on the menu bar and drag down to Subjects. This opens the subject listing for the database.
- Scroll through the Subjects. Double click on the selected subject to open citations. Click detailed display box for complete citation.

Analytical
- To begin an analytical search, select the type of search: Search Summary Fields by Keywords, Search Magazine by Keywords, Search date range, or Combine Previous Search Results by Keyword.
- Select Search Summary Fields by Keywords. Enter keywords. Mark the check box if Full Text is desired. Boolean operators (And, But Not) are available, and Or may be added to a search line along with truncation and wildcard operators. Proximity is indicated by [ ]. Click Search button. Results list opens. Double click citation to see more complete information or full text.
- Search Magazine by Keyword should be used for a simple search. Enter keyword and click Search button. This search finds citations that contain word or phrases in title. Results list opens.
- Search Date Range allows the searcher to enter a date range.
- To Combine Previous Search Results, select Search 1/Search 2. Click Search button and Results list will open.

Masterplots Complete

Publisher: Salem Press
Date: 1997
Grade Level: M- A
Brief Description: An electronic reference utilizing 21 sets of reference books from the print version of *Masterplots*. Entries are based on critical essays, character descriptions, and author biographies.
Printing: Printing available by clicking File on the menu bar. Drag down to Print or select the printer icon on the tool bar.

Format: Macintosh / MPC CD
Review based on Macintosh
Help: Question mark button on the tool bar.
Note taking: User annotation available by clicking on Pencil icon on the tool bar.

Explore
- Begin exploring by selecting Open Bookshelf from the File menu.
- Once a Bookshelf is loaded, explore the various options presented on the tool bar or menu bar.

Browse
- To begin a browse search, select Tools from the menu bar and click on Show Index area to open Index Box, Search Box, and Book Box.
- Index Box opens with options to search on Title, Author, Text, Locale, Genre, Subject, Principal Characters, and User Notes.
- Next select Books to search in the Book box.
- After selecting type of index and books to search within, enter topic to search. Topic will be located within alphabetical index.
- Double click topic to open information.

Hierarchical
- Not available.

Analytical
- To begin an analytical search, select Tools from the menu bar and click on Search or click on the Magnifying Glass on the tool bar.
- A search box will open which allows the searcher to use Wildcards, Match Case, Match Accents and select the Index type to use. Boolean operators (AND, OR, NOT) are available.
- Enter search term into search box and click Search. The Results window will open with a list of items from the search.

- Cross referencing is available by highlighting the word or name and clicking cross reference button (the eye) on the tool bar.
- Find feature available by selecting Tools from menu bar and clicking on Find or using the Find button on the tool bar. This will find word(s) within the text.

Mayo Clinic Family Health

Publisher: IVI Publishing
Date: 1997
Grade Level: M-A
Brief Description: Explores diseases and disorders; health and medication; emergency and accident care; anatomy; wellness; and physiological characteristics through an age timeline. Includes an update and search function online.

Printing:
Format: CD
Review based on: Windows
Help: Located on the top Menu Bar.
Note taking: Not available

Explore
- Words in articles make hypertext connections to other articles.
- Topical areas [Anatomy, Wellness, Timeline, Health Manager, Safety, and Medicine] represented by buttons across the top of the screen open lists of related articles.

Browse
- Select Search from Menu Bar across the top of screen.
- Browse Search choices include Illustration List, Dictionary, and Diseases and Disorders.
- Selection of Illustration List or Dictionary opens an alphabetical list of topics. Select topic to open an illustration or definition.
- Selection of Diseases and Disorders opens a window with a Search Box and scrollable index.
- Enter a topic in the Search Box. The index shifts to display the topic.
- Click on the topic to highlight and click on the Show Selected Topic button to open article.

Hierarchical
- Select a general topic from the topic bar across the top of the screen.
- Selection of specific topics from the topic box opens article.

Analytical
- Select Search from the Menu Bar. Enter word or phrase in Search box. Click on Search button.
- Search Results screen opens. Click on article number to open article.

Microsoft Bookshelf 98

Publisher: Microsoft Corp.
Date: 1998
Grade Level: E-A
Brief Description: An electronic reference library that includes: American Heritage Dictionary, Roget's Thesaurus, Columbia Dictionary of Quotations, Encarta 98 Desk Encyclopedia, Encarta 98 Desk World Atlas, The People's Chronology, The World Almanac and Book of Facts 1997, Internet Directory 98, Computer & Internet Dictionary, and Quick Zip Code Information. Online access available.

Printing: Open File on the Main Menu and select Print Article.
Format: CD
Review based on: Windows
Help: Available on the Menu Bar.
Note taking: Copy to Word and Copy to PowerPoint available under Edit on the Menu Bar.

Explore
- Articles include words that make hypertext connections to related information in other articles.

Browse
- Choose All Books or make a specific selection from the list of available books in the drop down menu.
- Select the Articles About option to search through a list of subjects and article titles.
- Enter a word or phrase in the Search Box. The list of article titles and subjects that appears in the index below shifts as letters are typed. When the subject appears, click to open detailed list. Click on specific article to open.

Hierarchical
- Not available.

Analytical
- Select the option All Articles Containing the Word(s).
- For a simple search, enter a word or phrase in the Search Box. Press Enter or click the Search Now button.
- Click on article title in results list to open.
- For a complex search, enter a word or phrase connected to another word or phrase with a Boolean operator [AND, OR, NOT, NEAR].
- Enclose an exact wording phrase in quotation marks.
- Press Enter or click the Search Now button.

- Results list appears in order of relevance with number of hits at the top.
- Click on article title to open.
- To further narrow the search click on the Advanced Search button.
- Select specific book and/or media type where appropriate.

Microsoft Encarta Encyclopedia 97

Publisher: Microsoft Corporation
Date: 1997
Grade Level: E-A
Brief Description: A multimedia encyclopedia that includes a dictionary, atlas, timeline, and updates via the Web.
Printing: Available under Options on the top menu bar. Printing options include: text selection, whole article, image/frame, and caption.

Format: CD
Review based on Windows
Help: Select the question mark (?) from the top menu bar.
Note taking: Notemarks feature located under Features then Tools. A specified word processor can be used under Tools also. Text, images, and charts can be copied.

Explore

- Four features allow exploration of many topics: Media Gallery, Interactivities, Collages, and Mindmaze. The Timeline and Atlas contain many hot spots (buttons and text) that make hyperlink connections to encyclopedia articles.
- To explore these features, select Features from the top menu bar, and next select Media Features. A pull down menu includes the Explore features. Select one and begin exploring.

Browse

- Selecting Find from the top menu bar opens the Pinpointer. The browse search feature is the default search option.
- Enter a word in the Search Box. The list of article titles that appears below will shift as letters are typed. When the search word appears, double click to open the article.

Hierarchical

- To conduct a Hierarchical Search, select Find from the top menu bar and the Pinpointer box appears on the screen.
- Click on Category to open the hierarchical list. Click on one of the nine Areas of Interest menu that opens to the right.

- Selection of an Area of Interest opens a Category list to the right. The two lists are the color coded for visible connection.
- Another very specific list of words appears on the left side of the screen. Clicking on the appropriate word opens an article.
- To return to the Category search screen, click on the Pinpointer button on the right side of the title bar.
- To begin a new search click on the Start Over button.

Analytical

- Select Find from the top menu bar and the Pinpointer appears on the screen.
- Click on Start Over to clear a previous search history.
- Click on Word Search.

- For a simple search click in the circle beside first Search Box and enter a word. Click on the Search button. Click on article title from list to open.
- For a complex search click on the circle beside the double Search boxes for a Boolean search using AND. Enter word in each Search box and click on Search button. Click on article title from list to open.
- For a complex search using all Boolean operators, phrases, or truncation click on the third option click on the circle beside the bottom box. Click on the Hints button and read the directions. Enter words or phrases in Search box. Click on article title from list to open.
- To return to the Pinpointer after opening an article select the Pinpointer icon on the right side of title bar.

Microsoft Encarta Encyclopedia 98

Publisher: Microsoft Corporation
Date: 1998
Grade Level: E-A
Brief Description:
A multimedia encyclopedia that includes a dictionary, atlas, and timeline with links to more than 10,000 Web resources.
Printing: Available under Options on the top menu bar. Printing options include: text selection, whole article, image/frame, and caption.

Format: CD
Review based on Windows
Help: Select the question mark (?) from the top menu bar. Help for searching is also available under Hints on the Word Search screen.
Note taking: Notemarks feature located under Features then Tools. A specified word processor can be used under Tools. Text, images, and charts can be copied.

Explore

- Four features allow exploration of many topics: Media Gallery, InterActivities, Interactive Collages, and a Mindmaze game. The Timeline and Atlas contain many hot spots (buttons and text) that make hyperlink connections to encyclopedia articles.
- To explore these features, select Features from the top menu bar, and select Media Features. A pull down menu includes these Explore features. To open click on one feature and begin exploring.

Browse

- Selecting Find from the top menu bar opens the Pinpointer. The browse search feature is the default search option.
- Click on New Search button to clear previous search.

- Enter a word or phrase in the Search Box. The list of article titles and subjects that appears in the index below shifts as letters are typed. When the selected title or subject appears, click to open.
- To filter the title and subject index by media type, date, or place, click on the Multimedia, Time, or Place buttons.

Hierarchical

- To conduct a Hierarchical Search, select Find from the top menu bar and the Pinpointer box appears on the screen.
- Click on New Search button to clear previous search.
- Click on Category to open the Areas of Interest list. Click on one of the nine areas to open a list of categories.
- The selected Area of Interest and related Category list are

color coded for visible connection.

- The Area of Interest and Category selections cause the title list to narrow. Clicking on the appropriate title opens an article. The status of results is located at the bottom of the index box.
- To return to the Category search screen, click on the Pinpointer button located on the right side of the title bar.
- To begin a new search click on the New Search button.

Analytical

- Select Find from the top menu bar and the Pinpointer menu box appears on the screen.
- Click on Start Over to clear a previous search history.
- Click on the Word Search button.
- For a simple search click in the circle beside first Search

Box and enter a word. Click on the Search button. Click on article title from list to open.

- For a complex search, click on the circle beside the double Search boxes for a Boolean search using AND. Enter word in each Search box and click on Search button. Click on article title from list to open.
- For a complex search using all Boolean operators, phrases, or truncation click in the circle beside the third option. Click on the Hints button and read the instructions. Enter words or phrases in Search box. Click on article title from list to open.
- The status of the results list is shown at bottom of index box.
- To return to the Pinpointer after opening an article select the Pinpointer icon on the right side of title bar.

Microsoft Encarta Virtual Globe

Publisher: Microsoft
Date: 1997
Grade Level: E-A
Brief Description: A multimedia atlas and gazetteer that includes articles, global statistics, virtual world flights, and place geography game. Connects to Web sites.
Printing: Print feature located under Options on top main menu. Prints maps, pictures, captions, and tables.

Format: CD
Review based on: Windows
Help: Select the question mark (?) from the top menu bar. Help for searching also available under Hints on Contents Find screen.
Note taking: Not available

Explore

- Explore features available from menu on start up screen include: View the World (opens globe), Learn About the Earth (articles on world themes), Play Name that Place, Take a World Flight. Click to open.
- Globe, maps, articles, and picture captions have hypertext links. Click on text to link to other information.
- Articles contain list of hyperlinks to related topics or articles.

Browse

- Click Find on top menu bar. Select from Places, Countries, World Music, World Themes, and Videos. Find box opens.
- Type article title in Search Box or click on title after scrolling through titles in index list.
- Click on article title to open.

Hierarchical

- Click Find on the top menu bar and select World Stats.
- Find box opens. Select from Category list and related type of World Stat.
- Select from statistical display on world map or table by clicking on buttons at bottom edge of screen.

Analytical

- Click Find on top menu bar and select Contents.
- Find box opens.
- Click on Hints button to review Boolean search options.
- For a simple search, type word or phrase in Search Box. Click on Find button. Article list changes to show search results. Click on specific article to open.
- For a complex search, use Boolean operators (and, or, not, near) to join words or phrases in Search Box. Click on Find button. Article list changes to show search results. Click on specific article to open.

Middle Search Plus

Publisher: EBSCO
Date: 1997
Grade Level: M-A
Brief Description: Includes three databases: Middle Search Plus, Colliers Encyclopedia, and Encyclopedia of Animals. Middle Search Plus searches through periodical references producing hit lists that include citations with abstracts and some full text articles.
Printing: Print marked citations or full text by selecting Print button on top of screen.

Format: CD
Review based on: Windows
Help: Help available on the top Menu Bar.
Note taking: Highlight text. Use the Copy function under Edit menu. Open word processor program and use the Paste function to position text in document.

Explore

- Only available in the Colliers Encyclopedia database. Articles contain text that hyperlink to other articles.

Browse

- Select a specific database by clicking on the Database button at bottom of initial screen. Click on database title to select then click on the Close button.
- For a Browse Search, select Subjects Middle button from top of screen.
- Type word in search box and press Enter or click on the Search button; or scroll the subject list.
- Subjects include number of available articles. Press Space Bar to make a list, or double click to view the Results list related to that subject.
- Citations can be viewed with a brief or full record by selecting button at bottom of screen.
- Double click on a record for full text of the article, where available.

Hierarchical

- Not available.

Analytical

- Click on the Start Over button at bottom of screen to clear previous search parameters.
- Select a database by clicking on the Database button.
- Enter word or phrase in Search Box and press Enter; or click on the Search button.
- Combine words and/or phrases by using Boolean operators: AND, OR, NOT.
- To narrow search, select date range, full text only option, or specific periodical.

- Use spacebar (or press the F key) to select titles for a list. Click on Full or Brief buttons to change citation option.
- Double click on specific article citation for full text option when available.

Mindscape STUDENT Reference Library

Publisher: Mindscape
Date: 1996
Grade Level: M -A
Brief Description: An electronic reference library accessing *Concise Columbia Electronic Encyclopedia, Reader's Companion to American History, 1996 Information Please Almanac, American Heritage Dictionary of the English Language, Enhanced Roget's Thesaurus, Dictionary of Cultural Literacy, Simpson's Contemporary Quotations, The Written Word III, Mindscape World Atlas, Limited Edition, Mindscape U.S. Atlas, Limited Edition.* Online access is also available.

Printing: Printing of text and pictures is available by clicking Menu on the Article Tool bar and pulling down to Print.
Format: Macintosh / MPC CD
Review based on Macintosh
Help: Help is available on the menu bar.
Note taking: Note taking is available by clicking Menu on the Article Tool bar and pulling down to Copy Article. Article will be copied to the clipboard and may be pasted into a word processor.

Explore

- Begin exploring with the Go Find It! option. Go Find It! asks a pertinent question and the searcher has the option to open the article and find the answer.
- Continue exploring by opening the various books available for searching to see what topics are listed.
- Try out the Menu, Photo, and Online buttons. Click and hold the buttons to see a listing of available information. The Online button will connect the searcher to a Lycos search of the topic.

Browse

- To begin a browse search, select a book to search within. Searcher may pick all books or select one or several.
- Next select Search and then the Search Type as Index from the tool bar.
- Then select Standard, Contains, Ends With or Starts With and enter a search term. Use of wildcard (*) is available for Index searching. Spell checking is available by clicking the Spell Check button. Click Find It! Search results open, double click to open article.

Hierarchical

- To begin an hierarchical search, click Contents on the tool bar and select a book to open. Contents of the almanac, the style guide, the quotations and literacy book are available. Click on the book's letter to open the contents.
- Select Level 1, 2, or 3 to view the contents in increasing depth. Double click a topic to open the article.

Analytical

- To begin an analytical search, select the books to search within.
- Next select Search and then the Search Type as Full-Text search.
- Then select Whole Word or Contains and enter the search term. Boolean operators may be used here. Spell checking is available by clicking the Spell Check button. Click Find It! Search results open, double click to open article.
- Quick Search is available by double clicking on any word within an open article. A results list will open. Select an entry to open the article.

Mindscape U.S. Atlas and Almanac

Publisher: Mindscape
Date: 1996
Grade Level: I - A
Brief Description: An electronic multimedia atlas and almanac with detailed full-color relief topographic, statistical, and political maps.
Printing: Printing of text and pictures is available by clicking on the Printer icon on the tool bar.

Format: Macintosh / Windows 3.1/MPC CD
Review based on Macintosh
Help: Help (?) is available on the menu bar.
Note taking: Note taking is available by selecting the Copier icon on the tool bar. Information can then be pasted to a word processor.

Explore

- Begin exploring by clicking and holding the continent map on the tool bar. A menu opens with County, Index, Relief, Satellite, Specialty, Topographical, Layer, and Slide Show as options. Select the type of map to view.
- To change the place, click and hold on the Star button at the top of the Main Window to select a state to view. Once a state is open, click the Star button at the bottom of the Main Window to open County or City information related to the state.
- Then click and hold the Globe button to select the statistical or pictorial information to view.

- Select the Accessory Windows to change and view information in smaller windows.

Browse

- To begin a browse search, click the Globe button and pull down to Search Index.
- An alphabetical listing will open with a search box. Enter a search term and click the Find button. A list of search results will open. Double click to view map.
- To view statistical information about the selection, click the Globe button and select City Information, County Information, or State Information. Additional options are available under the Globe button.

Hierarchical

- Not available.

Analytical

- Not available.

My First Incredible Amazing Dictionary

Publisher: Dorling Kindersley Multimedia
Date: 1995
Grade Level: E
Brief Description: An electronic dictionary of over 1,000 first words with their meanings.
Printing: Printing of text and pictures is available by clicking on Options and selecting Print from the menu.

Format: Macintosh / MPC CD
Review based on Macintosh
Help: Help for Parents is available from the Options button.
Note taking: Copying definitions is available through the Options button and selecting Copy.

Explore	Browse	Hierarchical	Analytical
• Begin exploring by clicking on anything Red as the directions suggest. • Another good Explore avenue is to select the Surprise Me button. A word opens that will allow the searcher to understand the sounds and links for each word in the dictionary.	• To begin a browse search, click an alphabet letter to open words and pictures associated with that letter. • Select a word and double click to open the definition. Click on the horn to hear the pronunciation and definition. • Red highlighted words link the searcher to other words related to the search word. • Another browse search method is to click on Quick Search. • Quick Search opens an alphabetical list of all the words in the dictionary The searcher may enter a word in the search box. Then click the Go box to open the definition of the word.	• A form of hierarchical searching is available once a word is opened. Topics related to the word are listed. • Double click to open the topic which lists words with pictures that are related to the topic. This gives the searcher a better understanding of how word groups are related.	• Not available.

National Geographic: The 90s

Publisher: National Geographic Interactive
Date: 1997
Grade Level: E-A
Brief Description: Includes every article and photograph from 1990-1996 issues. Photographs can be enlarged to fit the full screen and rotated for vertical and horizontal views.
Printing: Prints in black and white or color from Print button on bottom menu bar on article pages.

Format: CD-ROM
Review based on: Windows
Online Help: Help available in context of function or feature. Select Help button from menu bar or Hints button in various functions.
Online Note taking: Not available

Explore

- Selection of Content Menu on the menu bar opens a screen of National Geographic issue covers, year by year. Selection of a specific year and issue produces an enlargement of the cover or the table of contents. Article titles allow a hyperlink connection to the full article.
- To read an article, select the Zoom button on the bottom left side of screen. Use the enlarge button so the article fills the screen. The cursor becomes a hand which moves the page around so all text and pictures are visible.

Browse

- Select Search from the menu bar.
- When the Search screen opens, select List of Topics button at bottom left of screen.
- Click Titles for a list of article titles; or
- Click Related Topics and Contributors for a subject list.
- Enter words in search box or select a letter from the A, B, C, etc., list.
- Text box opens a list of titles or subjects.
- To view the article select the appropriate title or subject.

Hierarchical

- Not available.

Analytical

- Select Search from menu bar.
- For a simple search, enter a word or phrase in the search dialog box. Click Start. A selection list opens
- Highlight topic of interest and click Go to Selection button to see article.
- Click Search Results button on menu bar to return to results screen.
- For a complex search, enter a search phrase into the search dialog box. Connect words or phrases using the Boolean operators AND, OR, NOT, WITHOUT.
- Enclose phrases in quotation marks or brackets.

- Word Proximity choices allows searchers to use NEARx or ADJx.
- Filters provide the option to search every issue or a range of issues by date.

New Millennium World Atlas Deluxe

Publisher: Rand McNally New Media
Date: 1998
Grade Level: E-A
Brief Description: Includes 3-D maps, thematic maps, city center street maps, and geographic articles. Articles contain information on over 200 countries and territories. Links to resources on the Web.
Printing: Select Print from File on the top Menu Bar. Prints text and maps.

Format: CD
Review based on: Windows
Online Help: Select Help from the top Menu Bar; Locate topics from Contents or Find.
Online Note taking: Select the Notebook button on the bottom of the screen. Saves multiple notebooks by topic with maps, text, and pictures.

Explore

- Select Nature, Heritage, and Guidebook from the GeoLink buttons which connects to lists of button links of video clips, pictures, audio clips, and text.
- Text contains links to other articles and maps. Countries, cities, geographic features on maps link to other maps.

Browse

- To begin a Browse Search, select Find from the top Menu Bar or Global Find from the GeoLink menu.
- Find opens a subject list with a search box to input a word or phrase.
- Browse Search can be limited by selecting Maps and Information, Maps only, or Information only.

Hierarchical

- Not available.

Analytical

- Not available.

NewsBank Infoweb

Publisher: NewsBank, Inc.
Date: 1998
Grade Level: I -A
Brief Description: Online access to primary sources from around the world through full-text information from 500 domestic newspapers, government and international sources.
Printing: Printing is available by selecting File from the menu bar and dragging down to Print, or by selecting the Printer icon on the browser tool bar.

Format: Online
Review based on Online
Help: Help is available on search screens.
Note taking: Information may be highlighted and copied, then pasted to a word processor.

Explore
- Begin exploring at the main entry screen. Select either NewsFile Collection, News Headlines or Maps to learn more about this resource.

Browse
- To begin a browse search, select News Headlines.
- The searcher will be able to view Top Stories or the Monthly Archive of Headlines.
- Click article link to open article.
- Another browse search would be to select Maps. This will open a world map and the searcher may select an area to view. Topographic and political maps are also available.

Hierarchical
- Not available.

Analytical
- To begin an analytical search, select NewsFile Collection. This will open a keyword search.
- Searcher may enter a search request into the search strategy box. Boolean operators AND, OR, NOT may be used. Search results will be returned in relevance order.
- Results list returns articles listed by Rank, Date, Source and Link to Headline. Select the Link to Headline to open the article.

- The searcher may select Customized Search for a more in-depth search.
- Search strategy boxes open allowing the searcher to type in a phrase in quotation marks or several terms. The searcher must select AND, OR, NOT along with selecting to search in All Text, Topics, Lead/First Paragraph, Headline/Title, Source, or Source Type. The searcher may also select a date range in which to search. Click Search.
- Results list returns articles found in reverse chronological order.

Picture Atlas of the World

Publisher: National Geographic Society
Date: 1995
Grade Level: E - A
Brief Description: An interactive atlas of more than 800 political and physical maps of the world, the oceans, the continents, regions, nations, transportation networks, cultural and historical sites.
Printing: Printing of text and pictures isavailable by clicking on File on the menu bar and dragging down to Print.

Format: Macintosh / MPC CD
Review based on Macintosh
Help: Not available.
Note taking: Note taking is available by highlighting sections of the text. Click Edit on menu bar and drag down to Copy. Paste to a resident word processor.

Explore

- Begin exploring by selecting Guided Tour from the opening menu. This opens an explanation of the various buttons available to the searcher.
- Continue browsing by selecting Mapping Our World from the opening menu. This is an explanation of how cartographers create maps.

Browse

- To begin a browse search, select World Atlas from the opening menu.
- This allows the searcher to pick a continent by clicking on the arrows around the globe or select Index.
- The Index allows the searcher to select a topic alphabetically by continent, by continent and country, and alphabetically by country.
- The searcher selects how to search and then highlights their request on the alphabetical listing. Click Go There to open the information. A red arrow points out the site selected. Clicking the Media button will open Flag, Photo, Video, Speech, Music, Essay and Stats buttons for additional information.

Hierarchical

- Not available.

Analytical

- Not available.

ProQuest Direct

Publisher: UMI
Date: 1998
Grade Level: P -A
Brief Description: Online access to 1800 publications with 500 full-text including newspapers, journals, periodicals, magazines, and other sources.
Printing: Printing is available by selecting File from the menu bar and dragging down to Print, or by selecting the Printer icon on the browser tool bar. Articles may also be emailed.

Format: Online
Review based on Online
Help: Help is a button on every screen.
Note taking: Information may be highlighted and copied, then pasted to a word processor.

Explore

- Begin exploring at the main entry screen, using the Intro or Help buttons. The Intro button has a Scavenger Hunt for the beginning user to try.
- Selecting the UMI Jeep icon takes the searcher to the UMI information page.
- Continue exploring by selecting either the Search by Word button, one of the topics in Search by Topic, or the Topics for Teachers link.

Browse

- To begin a browse search, select the Search By Word button. This opens a basic search strategy box. The searcher may enter a search term. Terms may be combined by using And. Click the Search button.

- A results listing will open and the searcher may select to see the listing by full-text only. Articles are listed in chronological order, and indicate whether a citation, abstract, full-text, text + graphics, and page image are available.
- Click article link to open article.
- Another browse search would be to select the Search by Publication button. This will search for words in the title of a publication.

Hierarchical

- The main screen is the entrance to Search by Topic. Topic listings such as Health, Plants, Animals, Social Studies, Sports and Entertainment, The Arts, Critical Issues, In the News, People, Earth Science,

Technology and Industry are available.
- Select a topic by clicking on it. A subtopic screen opens. The searcher may continue to select subtopics until a listing of article choices opens.
- Select a link for an article to open it. At the bottom of each article is a link to how to cite the article in a bibliography.

Analytical

- To begin an analytical search, select the Search By Word button and then the Advanced Search button.
- A search strategy box with up to four terms will open. Boolean combinations of And, Or, And Not, Within 3 may be selected.

- The searcher may also select to search in All Fields, Article, Title, Author, Company, Geographical Name, Personal Name, Publication Title, Subject, or Text. The searcher may select a Date Rangeand Search Options.
- Click the Search button. A results listing will open and the searcher may select to see the listing by full-text only. Articles are listed in chronological order, and indicate whether a citation, abstract, full-text, text + graphics, and page image are available.
- Click the article link to open the article.

ProQuest IssueQuest

Publisher: UMI
Date: 1997
Grade Level: M -A
Brief Description: Electronic issue-based resourcecontaining thousands of full-text newspaper articles covering key topics researched in schools.
Printing: Selecting the F4 command will open the Print/Save screen.

Format: Win/MPC CD
Review based on MPC
Help: Select F1 Key for Help.
Note taking: Information may be highlighted and copied, then pasted to a word processor.

Explore

- Begin exploring by pressing any key at the main screen to enter IssueQuest.
- Read through the online explanation of the software and its setup.

Browse

- Not available.

Hierarchical

- At the main search screen, select Topic Search.
- Type into the search strategy box a topic to search. An alphabetical listing by topic with subtopic choices will open. The number of articles containing information on each topic is listed.
- An introduction to the topic is always the first article and then the related articles are listed. The Escape button takes the searcher back to the results list.
- If the topic requested is not in the topic database, the searcher is asked to search the entire database. If Yes is chosen, this will show all articles where the search word is mentioned.

Analytical

- To begin an analytical search, select Keyword Search.
- Searcher may enter keyword or keywords connected by Boolean operators. Examples are shown.
- The search results will be listed. Press enter to view titles and use F7 to view full records. The searcher may have several searches open at one time. Using the tab key allows the searcher to move between various searches.
- If the searcher has trouble formulating keywords to search, the program suggests using F6 to select words from various indexes. The software will combine these terms to search.

Reader's Guide for Young People

Publisher: H.W. Wilson
Date: 1997
Grade Level: E-S
Brief Description: An electronic periodical reference covering January, 1994 through July, 1997.
Printing: Printing of text is available by clicking File on the menu bar, dragging down to Print. A Print button is also available at the bottom of each citation.

Format: Macintosh / MPC CD
Review based on Macintosh
Help: Help is available on the menu bar and within each citation.
Note taking: Notetaking is available through the Save feature within each citation or by highlighting the text and copying. Open a word processor resident on the computer and paste the text.

Explore
- Not available.

Browse
- With the WilsonDiscs CD Rom Retrieval System, Browse is an immediate choice.
- Click the Browse button to open the alphabetical listing of search terms.
- Place the cursor in the search box, type in search term and click Display. Search term will be highlighted with number of citations in an alphabetical listing. Double click search term listing and the complete Citation will open. Select List from Citation Box tool bar for a complete list of Citations.
- To refine a Browse search, select the Category button to open an alphabetical listing for Subjects, All Terms, Broad Subjects, Movie TV Reviews, Book Reviews, or Topics for Teachers. Type in search term, select Browse.

Hierarchical
- Not available.

Analytical
- To begin an analytical search, click Keyword Search from the opening screen, or select Window on menu bar and drag down to Search: Keyword.
- Searcher has the option of typing in several search terms combined with And or And Not. Selecting Options on the tool bar allows additional search descriptors, such as Author or Subject,.
- Click Search and first Citation will open. Citation listing is available by clicking List on toolbar.

SIRS Discoverer

Publisher: SIRS, Inc.
Date: 1997
Grade Level: E - M
Brief Description: An interactive reference tool utilizing over 300 magazines, newspapers, and *The 1997 World Almanac for Kids*.
Printing: Available as a Printer icon on the top tool bar of each article.

Format: Macintosh /Windows/ MPC CD
Review based on Macintosh
Help: Command / to open the help screen.
Note taking: Note taking is available by selecting the Note taking button on the tool bar of each article.

Explore

- Begin exploring by looking through each of the subjects listed in the main window.
- Continue exploring by opening *The 1997 World Almanac for Kids*.

Browse

- To begin a browse search, click the Subject Headings button.
- If the searcher just wishes to browse the subject index, click Cancel when the search term box appears. This will open an alphabetical listing of subjects. Highlight a topic and click OK to see a listing of articles.
- To continue Browse searching, select a Subject Heading Search. Type in a simple subject

heading and Click Search. This will locate the subject searched within an alphabetical listing of subjects. Highlight a subject and click to see a listing of possible articles. Highlight an article to read and click OK to open the full text of the article.
- When browsing *The 1997 World Almanac for Kids*, open the Almanac and select the Table of Contents button. This opens an alphabetical listing. Double click the topic to open a results list.

Hierarchical

- To begin an hierarchical search, the searcher may select the subjects listed in the Main Window under the Subject Tree Searching option.
- Select a category button. Click to open a list of subtopics. Highlight the subtopic and click the OK button to either open more subtopics or an article.

Analytical

- To begin an analytical search, select the Keyword Search. buttons.
- Selecting Keyword Search, the searcher will get a search box that allows for entry of a single search word or multiples using Boolean operators AND, OR, NOT. Truncation with an asterisk is also available.
- Next, the searcher should select the Total button to see the combination results and the Ok button to view a listing of articles to open.
- To use *The World Almanac for Kids* for keyword searching, follow the same method as suggested above for Keyword Searching.

SIRS Researcher

Publisher: SIRS, Inc.
Date: 1997
Grade Level: J - S
Brief Description: An interactive reference tool utilizing over 1200 magazines, newspapers, government journals along with *Newsline*, *Directory of Publications*, and *Maps of the World*.
Printing: Available as a Printer icon on the top tool bar of each article.

Format: Macintosh /Windows/ MPC CD
Review based on Macintosh
Help: Command / to open the help screen.
Note taking: Note taking is available by selecting the Note taking button on the tool bar of each article.

Explore

- Begin exploring by seeing how the Subject Headings, Keyword Search and Topic Browse buttons work.
- Continue exploring by opening the *Newsline, Directory of Publications, and Maps of the World* buttons.

Browse

- To begin a browse search, click the Topic Browse button.
- An alphabetical listing of topics window opens. Highlight a topic and the year in which to search and click OK. A listing of article titles opens. Highlight the article and click Ok to open the full text.
- Continue browsing with a Subject Heading search. Type in a simple subject heading and click Search. This will locate the subject searched within an alphabetical listing of subjects. Highlight a subject and click to see a listing of possible articles. Highlight an article to read and click OK to open the full text of the article.

- Open the *Newsline* button and select Date Browse to look through historic happenings during a certain time period.
- Click *the Maps of the World* button and select one of the area buttons to view a listing of state or country maps.
- Select the *Directory of Publications* button to view an alphabetical listing and additional information of the various journals included in *Sirs Researcher*.

Hierarchical

- Not available.

Analytical

- To begin an analytical search, select the Keyword Search button.
- Selecting Keyword Search, the searcher will get a search box that allows for entry of a single search word or multiples using Boolean operators AND, OR, NOT. Truncation with an asterisk is also available.
- Next, the searcher should select the Total button to see the combination results and the Ok button to view a listing of articles to open.
- To use *Newsline* for subject heading searching, follow the same method as suggested above for Subject Heading searching.

TIME Magazine Multimedia Almanac

Publisher: Time, Inc./SoftKey Multimedia, Inc.
Date: 1995
Grade Level: M-S
Brief Description: An electronic reference tool that contains text, audio, video, charts, maps and statistical data along with information on historical events from the 1900's through 1995 and weekly *TIME Magazine* articles from 1989 to 1995. There is also an online connection through *America Online* to the Time Warner's Pathfinder homepage.

Printing: Printing of text and pictures is available by selecting the Print button on the tool bar.
Format: Macintosh / WIN / MPC CD
Review based on MPC
Help: Help is available on the tool bar.
Note taking: Note taking is available from the Notes button on the tool bar.

Explore
- Begin exploring by selecting the various TIME covers dealing with the specific topics of Environment, Elections, Cyberspace, Diversity, Portfolio, Almanac and the game News Quest.
- Continue exploring by selecting the *America Online* button from the tool bar. Open the online connection to the Pathfinder homepage to view current *TIME Magazine* articles.

Browse
- To begin a browse search, select Search from the tool bar.
- A search box will open that the searcher may type in a search term or browse the alphabetical order index.
- The searcher must also select media to include in a search and decide whether to search by a word or a phrase. Select Results button to view listings. Highlight and click an article to open.

Hierarchical
- To begin an hierarchical search, select a topic from one of the magazine covers on the opening screen. This will lead the searcher to subtopics which when chosen will open a list of possible articles. Highlight and click to open the selected article.

Analytical
- To begin an analytical search, select the Search button from the tool bar.
- Select the Advanced Search button. Enter a search term using Boolean operators and limiters. Examples of allowed search operators are shown below the search box. Click OK.
- A results list will open. Highlight an article and click to open, or select the Search button to return to the search box.
- A search button is also available through the online connection at pathfinder.com.

Ultimate Children's Encyclopedia

Publisher: The Learning Company
Date: 1996
Grade Level: E-J
Brief Description: A multimedia reference library that includes an encyclopedia, dictionary, thesaurus, atlas, book of words, and more. Online access to Compton's Living Encyclopedia through America Online.
Printing: Available from Print button on top of screen.

Format: CD
Review based on: Windows
Help: Available from the Help button on the Menu Bar.
Note taking: The Journal button opens a note taking feature. Copy words or images into Wordpad or a designated word processor.

Explore

- The start up screen is a boy's bedroom loaded with images that link to articles, pictures, sound and video clips. Click on any hot spot to find many interesting topics to explore.
- Moving cursor over objects opens a label to identify the buttons in the room. Click on button of choice to open.
- Screen opens with new image hotspots and a list of topics. Click to open.
- Click on the All About Words button on the Menu Bar to explore words in the form of quotations, jokes, wise or famous sayings.

Browse

- Click on the Find button on the start up screen. The Multimedia and Article buttons open indexes. Multimedia indexes the various media [video, pictures, sound clips, etc.] and Article indexes all the articles.
- Click on either the Multimedia or Article button to open.
- Type word or words in the Search Box.
- Click on title to open.
- For a phrase search, click on the Idea button. Enter a word, phrase, or short sentence query in the Search Box and press Enter.
- Click on a topic from the list to open article.

Hierarchical

- Select Topic from the Find menu on the start up page.
- Click on one of the 19 broad topics.
- Click on subtopic when next screen appears.
- Click on article title to open.

Analytical

- Open the Find menu and click on the All button.
- Enter a word or words in the Search Box using Boolean operators [and, or, not]. Press Enter to begin search.
- Click on title in results list to open.

U*X*L Biographies

Publisher: Gale Research, Inc.
Date: 1996
Grade Level: M- A
Brief Description: An electronic resource for biographies and portraits of 1500 high-interest people.
Printing: Print button available on biography screen. Searchers may print full biography or brief biography.

Format: Macintosh/Win CD
Review based on Macintosh
Help: Help is available as a button on each screen.
Note taking: Biographies may be saved to disk, or parts marked and then saved.

Explore

- Begin exploring at the main menu screen by selecting Name, Subject Term, Personal Data, or Custom Search buttons to see how the CD operates.

Browse

- To begin a browse search, the searcher may select Name or Subject Term from the main menu screen.
- Once the search screen for each section opens, searchers are able to input their search request or select from the alphabetical listing. The search term is highlighted within the listing. Use the Select Name or Search Now button to open the selection.

Hierarchical

- Not available.

Analytical

- To begin an analytical search, select the Custom Search button from the main menu. Type in a search term by word(s) or phrases in quotation marks. Utilizes the Boolean operators AND, OR, NOT and truncation.
- Click the Search Now button. The number of search combinations will be displayed.
- Select the Display Names button to open the listing of possible search hits.
- Use the Personal Data button on the main menu to search for combinations of biographies. Entering combinations of birth, death, nationality, and other choices narrows the number of selections available. If the searcher needs help with selecting criteria, click the Personal Data item to open a selection of searchable terms to use in the search box.
- Select Display Names to open selections to search.

The Way Things Work 2.0

Publisher: Dorling Kindersley Multimedia
Date: 1996
Grade Level: E - A
Brief Description: An electronic reference for information about inventions and inventors. This CD utilizes a World Wide Web connection through mammoth.net.
Printing: Printing of text and pictures is available by clicking on Options and selecting Print.

Format: Macintosh / MPC CD
Review based on Macintosh
Help: Help is available by clicking on the Options button.
Note taking: Copying the immediate screen is available by selecting the Options button and then Copy Active Window.

Explore

- Begin exploring by clicking on any of the available buttons such as Warehouse, Machines , Principles, Inventions, Storeroom, Index, mammoth.net.
- These buttons take the searcher through various aspects of machines and inventions.
- Select mammoth.net to explore the online component.

Browse

- To begin a browse search, select Index. This opens a list of all the machines available for searching. Either select a machine by highlighting or type in the name of the machine. Click Ok and the information about the machine will open.
- To continue browsing, click on Machines. Machines opens the A-Z of Machines.
- Select a machine to view. Red highlighted words can be selected and a glossary definition will appear.
- The See Also buttons gives the searcher additional topics related to their subject.
- For another browse search option, click on Inventors. An alphabetical index opens. Select a letter of the alphabet to open a list of inventors. Double click on the inventor to open more information.

Hierarchical

- To begin an hierarchical search, click the Principles button.
- Principles opens a list of scientific principles. Select one to view information about the Principle and also information on other Related Machines.

Analytical

- Not available.

Wide World of Animals

Publisher: Creative Wonders/ABC Electronic Arts
Date: 1995
Grade Level: P -S
Brief Description: An electronic reference tool that explores world wildlife and their relationships.
Printing: Printing of text and pictures is available by selecting File and dragging down to Print.

Format: Macintosh / WIN / MPC CD
Review based on MPC
Help: Help is available on the Menu bar.
Note taking: Not available

Explore

- Begin exploring by selecting Contents from the menu bar. Open any of the menu options listed to see how the CD operates.
- Continue exploring by viewing the Find locator to see all the available areas to search.
- Select Glossary button to view definitions and see also relationships.

Browse

- To begin a browse search, select Browser from the Contents menu. Click a topic to open more information.
- Continue browsing by using the Find locator which is available on every screen.
- Find locator allows the searcher to type in a name of an animal to search for or highlight a animal name in the alphabetical listing. Searcher may select Mammals, Birds, Reptiles, Amphibians, Fish, and Threatened Animals.
- Double click to open article information. Use the Go Back button to return.

Hierarchical

- Not available.

Analytical

- To begin an analytical search, select Edit from the menu bar and drag down to Search.
- This will open a Keyword search. Searcher may type in a keyword. The keyword will be located within the index and will also show all the wildlife that apply to the keyword.
- Searcher may then highlight the location they would like to view and click the Go To button to open the information.

World Book 1997 Multimedia Encyclopedia

Publisher: IBM
Date: 1997
Grade Level: E-A
Brief Description: A multimedia encyclopedia that includes a dictionary, atlas, timeline, and Internet access to a Web site with additional information.
Printing: Available under the File menu on the Menu Bar or the Print icon in the article window.

Format: CD
Review based on: Windows
Help: Select Help from the Menu Bar.
Note taking: Available under Tools on the Menu Bar.

Explore

- Click on the Time Frame icon on the menu bar to open the timeline.
- Select the year, decade, century, millennium, or era from the icons at the bottom of the screen. To select an Era, click on the arrow to open a list of Eras, highlight and click on the Go button. To select a category, click on the year, decade, century, or millennium buttons.
- Click on the boxes on the timeline to open an article.
- Click on the Around the World button to explore geographic information. When maps appear, click on hot spots to zoom in on specific places. Click on places to open articles.

- Highlighting a word or phrase in the article text opens a dictionary definition.
- Clicking on the See Also topics in upper case letters at the end of articles opens other related articles.

Browse

- Not available.

Hierarchical

- Click on the Just Looking icon to open.
- Click on the arrow beside the Categories button and select a category.
- Clicking the arrow beside the Content button opens a list of formats that will narrow a search.
- Click on the Find button to open a list of articles related to the selected category.
- Double clicking on the article title opens the article.

Analytical

- Click on the Search button to open the Search window.
- The Topic Search feature enables a Simple Search.
- To begin the search enter a word or phrase in the search box. Click on the Go icon. Double click on an article in the window to open.
- The Word Search feature enables a Complex Search. Enter a word or phrase in the Word search boxes using AND, OR, or NOT as connecting Boolean operators. Click on the Go icon to begin the search. Double click on an article in the window to open.

World News CD-ROM

Publisher: Facts on File News Services.
Date: 1997
Grade Level: M-S
Brief Description: An online electronic reference tool that utilizes *Netscape Navigator* as its interface. This CD contains the full text of *Facts On File* since January 1, 1980.
Printing: Printing of text and pictures is available by selecting the Print button on the tool bar.

Format: Macintosh / WIN / MPC CD
Review based on MPC
Help: Help is available on the main menu.
Note taking: Note taking is available by highlighting the information and copying.

Explore

- Begin exploring from the opening screen by selecting Find News Stories by Keyword Search or Subject Index.
- Continue exploring by selecting Background to the News through Key Events, Key Issues or Key People.
- Another piece to explore is the Index to Documents, Maps and Photos.

Browse

- To begin a browse search, select either Key Events, Key Issues, or Key People. An alphabetical listing will open. Highlight and click to open link to the document.
- Another browse search is available by selecting Index to Documents, Maps, Photos.
- Continue browsing by clicking the Select Primary Source button. Next select Primary Source Arranged by Title or Arranged by Year. Select the document to open.
- If the searcher decides to Open Maps, an alphabetical listing is available by Regions, States, Provinces and Cities.

- The searcher may also Open News Photos and Portraits. This opens an alphabetical list arranged by People or Events and Objects.

Hierarchical

- To begin an hierarchical search, the searcher may click Subject Index Search from the main menu. Next select General Subject.
- This will open a subtopic listing which allows the searcher to continue selecting subtopics until a document opens.

Analytical

- To begin an analytical search, select Keyword Search from the main menu.
- The searcher may enter a topic or a question into the Keyword Search Box. Selection of optional date range, reverse chronological order or relevance rank order is available. Click the Search button.
- A results list will open and each entry is relevance ranked.
- Searchers may use Boolean operators. Single quotes should be used around an exact phrase.

Appendices

Bibliography

Bibliography

Anderson, Mary Alice. (Ed.). (1996). *Teaching information literacy using electronic resources, for grades 6-12.* Worthington, OH: Linworth Publishing.

Barclay, Donald. (1995). *Teaching electronic information literacy.* New York: Neal-Schuman.

California School Library Association. (1997). (2nd Edition). *From library skills to information literacy: A Handbook for the 21st century.* Castle Rock, CO: Hi Willow Research and Publishing.

Craver, Kathleen W. (1997). *Teaching electronic literacy: A Concepts-based approach for school library media specialists.* Westport, CT: Greenwood Press.

Dubin, David. (1995). Search strategies for Internet resources. *School Library Media Quarterly*, 24, 53-54.

Eisenberg, Michael B. and Robert E. Berkowitz. (1990). *Information problem solving: The Big six skills approach to library & information skills instruction.* Norwood, NJ: Ablex.

Harris, Judi. (1996). Telehunting, telegathering, teleharvesting: Information-seeking and information-synthesis on the Internet. *Learning and Leading with Technology*; 23 (4) 36-39.

Hyerle, David. *Visual tools for constructing knowledge.* Alexandria, VA: ASCD.

Jasco, P. (1992). *CD-ROM software, dataware, and hardware.* Englewood, CO: Libraries Unlimited.

Langhorne, M. J. (Ed.). (1998). *Developing an information literacy program K-12.* New York: Neal Schuman.

Marchionini, Gary. (1989). Information-seeking strategies of novices using a full-text electronic encyclopedia. *Journal of the American Society for Information Science*, 40, 54-66.

Marchionini, Gary. (1995). *Information seeking in electronic environments.* New York: Cambridge Press.

Pappas, Marjorie L. (1995). Analytical searching. *School Library Media Activities Monthly*, 12 (4), 35-37.

Pappas, Marjorie L. (1998). Common search strategies for print and electronic resources. *Technology Connection*, 5 (3).

Pappas, Marjorie L. (1996). Hypertext searching through electronic resources. *School Library Media Activities Monthly*, 12 (6), 38-39.

Pappas, Marjorie L. (1997). Organizing research. *School Library Media Activities Monthly*, 14, (4), 30-32.

Pappas, Marjorie L. & Ann E. Tepe. (1997). *Pathways to knowledge*™. (3ʳᵈ ed.). McHenry, IL: Follett Software Co.

Pfaffenberger, Bryan. (1996). *Web search strategies*. New York: MIS Press.

Skeele, Linda. (Ed.). (1996). *Teaching information literacy using electronic resources, for grades K-6*. Worthington, OH: Linworth Publishing.

Teaching electronic information skills: A Resource guide for grades K-5. McHenry, IL: Follett Software Co.

Teaching electronic information skills: A Resource guide for grades 6-8. McHenry, IL: Follett Software Co.

Teaching electronic information skills: A Resource guide for grades 9-12. McHenry, IL: Follett Software Co.

Publisher's Lists

Alphabetical List By Title

Title	Publisher	Type
3D Atlas 98	Creative Wonders	Reference/Atlas
ABC News Links	Creative Wonders	Social Studies
American Heritage Talking Dictionary	SoftKey International, Inc.	Reference/Dict
Bartlett's Familiar Quotations	Time Warner Electronic Publishing	Reference
Britannica OnLine	Encyclopeadia Britannica	Reference/Ency.
Cartopedia	DK Multimedia	Reference/Atlas
Collier's Encyclopedia 1998	Sierra Home	Reference/Ency.
Compton's Interactive Encyclopedia 1998	The Learning Company	Reference/Ency
Compton's Interactive World Atlas	Compton's NewMedia, Inc.	Reference/Atlas
Contemporary Authors on CD	Gale Publishing	Literature
Current Biography 1940-Present	H.W. Wilson	Reference
DISCovering U.S. History	Gale Publishing	Social Studies
DISCovering World History	Gale Publishing	Social Studies
Earth Quest	DK Multimedia	Science
Electric Library	Infonautics	Reference
Encarta '97 Encyclopedia	Microsoft	Reference/Ency
Encarta 98 Encyclopedia	Microsoft	Reference/Ency
Encyclopedia Americana on CD-ROM	Grolier Educational	Reference/Ency
Encyclopedia of Careers and Vocational Guidance	Ferguson Publishing	Guidance
Exegy	ABC-CLIO	Social Studies
Eyewitness Children's Encyclopedia	DK Multimedia	Reference/Ency
Eyewitness Encyclopedia of Nature	DK Multimedia	Science
Eyewitness History of the World	DK Multimedia	Social Studies
FIND IT! SCIENCE	Follett Software	Science
Grolier Multimedia Encyclopedia 1998	Grolier Interactive	Reference/Ency
Interactive Science CD-ROM	Steck Vaughn Company	Science
IssueQuest	UMI	Periodical

Landmark Documents in American History	Facts on File News Services	Reference
Mammals Multimedia Encyclopedia	National Geographic Society	Science
MAS Full Text Premier	Ebsco Publishing	Periodical
MasterPlots Complete	Salem Press	Literature
Mayo Clinic Family Health Book	IVI Publishing	Science
Microsoft Bookshelf 98	Microsoft	Reference
Microsoft Encarta Virtual Globe	Microsoft	Reference/Atlas
Middle Search	Ebsco Publishing	Periodical
Mindscape Student Reference Library	Mindscape	Reference
Mindscape U.S. Atlas and Almanac	Mindscape	Reference/Atlas
Mindscape World Atlas and Almanac	Mindscape	Reference/Atlas
My First Incredible Amazing Dictionary	DK Multimedia	Reference/Dict
National Geographic: The 90s	National Geographic Society	Periodical
New Millennium World Atlas Dexluxe	Rand McNally	Reference/Atlas
NewsBank Infoweb	NewsBank	Periodical
Picture Atlas of the World	National Geographic Society	Reference/Atlas
ProQuest Direct	UMI	Periodical
Reader's Guide for Young People	H.W. Wilson	Periodical
SIRS Discoverer	SIRS, Inc.	Reference
SIRS Researcher	SIRS, Inc.	Reference
The Way Things Work 2.0	DK Multimedia	Science
TIME Magazine Multimedia Almanac	SoftKey International, Inc.	Reference/Almanac
U*X*L Biographies	Gale Publishing	Reference
Ultimate Childrens' Encyclopedia	Learning Co.	Reference/Ency.
Wide World of Animals	Creative Wonders	Science
World Book 1997 Multimedia Encyclopedia	IBM	Reference/Ency
World News CD-ROM	Facts on File	Social Studies

Alphabetical List by Publisher

Publisher	Title	Type
ABC-CLIO	Exegy	Social Studies
Compton's NewMedia, Inc.	Compton's Interactive World Atlas	Reference/Atlas
Creative Wonders	3D Atlas 98	Reference/Atlas
Creative Wonders	ABC News Links	Social Studies
Creative Wonders	Wide World of Animals	Science
DK Multimedia	Cartopedia	Reference/Atlas
DK Multimedia	Earth Quest	Science
DK Multimedia	Eyewitness Children's Encyclopedia	Reference/Ency
DK Multimedia	Eyewitness Encyclopedia of Nature	Science
DK Multimedia	Eyewitness History of the World	Social Studies
DK Multimedia	My First Incredible Amazing Dictionary	Reference/Dict
DK Multimedia	The Way Things Work 2.0	Science
Ebsco Publishing	MAS Full Text Premier	Periodical
Ebsco Publishing	Middle Search	Periodical
Encyclopeadia Britannica	Britannica OnLine	Reference/Ency.
Facts on File	World News CD-ROM	Social Studies
Facts on File News Services	Landmark Documents in American History	Reference
Ferguson Publishing	Encyclopedia of Careers and Vocational Guidance	Guidance
Follett Software	FIND IT! SCIENCE	Science
Gale Publishing	Contemporary Authors on CD	Literature
Gale Publishing	DISCovering U.S. History	Social Studies
Gale Publishing	DISCovering World History	Social Studies
Gale Publishing	U*X*L Biographies	Reference
Grolier Educational	Encyclopedia Americana on CD-ROM	Reference/Ency
Grolier Interactive	Grolier Multimedia Encyclopedia 1998	Reference/Ency
H.W. Wilson	Current Biography 1940-Present	Reference
H.W. Wilson	Reader's Guide for Young People	Periodical

IBM	World Book 1997 Multimedia Encyclopedia	Reference/Ency
Infonautics	Electric Library	Reference
IVI Publishing	Mayo Clinic Family Health Book	Science
Learning Co.	Ultimate Childrens' Encyclopedia	Reference/Ency.
Microsoft	Encarta '97 Encyclopedia	Reference/Ency
Microsoft	Encarta 98 Encyclopedia	Reference/Ency
Microsoft	Microsoft Bookshelf 98	Reference
Microsoft	Microsoft Encarta Virtual Globe	Reference/Atlas
Mindscape	Mindscape Student Reference Library	Reference
Mindscape	Mindscape U.S. Atlas and Almanac	Reference/Atlas
Mindscape	Mindscape World Atlas and Almanac	Reference/Atlas
National Geographic Society	Mammals Multimedia Encyclopedia	Science
National Geographic Society	National Geographic: The 90s	Periodical
National Geographic Society	Picture Atlas of the World	Reference/Atlas
NewsBank	NewsBank Infoweb	Periodical
Rand McNally	New Millennium World Atlas Dexluxe	Reference/Atlas
Salem Press	MasterPlots Complete	Literature
Sierra Home	Collier's Encyclopedia 1998	Reference/Ency.
SIRS, Inc.	SIRS Discoverer	Reference
SIRS, Inc.	SIRS Researcher	Reference
SoftKey International, Inc.	American Heritage Talking Dictionary	Reference/Dict
SoftKey International, Inc.	TIME Magazine Multimedia Almanac	Reference/Almanac
Steck Vaughn Company	Interactive Science CD-ROM	Science
The Learning Company	Compton's Interactive Encyclopedia 1998	Reference/Ency
Time Warner Electronic Publishing	Bartlett's Familiar Quotations	Reference
UMI	IssueQuest	Periodical
UMI	ProQuest Direct	Periodical

Alphabetical List by Type

Type	Title	Publisher
Guidance	Encyclopedia of Careers and Vocational Guidance	Ferguson Publishing
Literature	Contemporary Authors on CD	Gale Publishing
Literature	MasterPlots Complete	Salem Press
Periodical	MAS Full Text Premier	Ebsco Publishing
Periodical	Middle Search	Ebsco Publishing
Periodical	Reader's Guide for Young People	H.W. Wilson
Periodical	National Geographic: The 90s	National Geographic Society
Periodical	NewsBank Infoweb	NewsBank
Periodical	IssueQuest	UMI
Periodical	ProQuest Direct	UMI
Reference	Landmark Documents in American History	Facts on File News Services
Reference	U*X*L Biographies	Gale Publishing
Reference	Current Biography 1940-Present	H.W. Wilson
Reference	Electric Library	Infonautics
Reference	Microsoft Bookshelf 98	Microsoft
Reference	Mindscape Student Reference Library	Mindscape
Reference	SIRS Discoverer	SIRS, Inc.
Reference	SIRS Researcher	SIRS, Inc.
Reference	Bartlett's Familiar Quotations	Time Warner Electronic Publishing
Reference/Almanac	TIME Magazine Multimedia Almanac	SoftKey International, Inc.
Reference/Atlas	Compton's Interactive World Atlas	Compton's NewMedia, Inc.
Reference/Atlas	3D Atlas 98	Creative Wonders
Reference/Atlas	Cartopedia	DK Multimedia
Reference/Atlas	Microsoft Encarta Virtual Globe	Microsoft
Reference/Atlas	Mindscape U.S. Atlas and Almanac	Mindscape
Reference/Atlas	Mindscape World Atlas and Almanac	Mindscape
Reference/Atlas	Picture Atlas of the World	National Geographic Society

Reference/Atlas	New Millennium World Atlas Dexluxe	Rand McNally
Reference/Dict	My First Incredible Amazing Dictionary	DK Multimedia
Reference/Dict	American Heritage Talking Dictionary	SoftKey International, Inc.
Reference/Ency	Eyewitness Children's Encyclopedia	DK Multimedia
Reference/Ency	Encyclopedia Americana on CD-ROM	Grolier Educational
Reference/Ency	Grolier Multimedia Encyclopedia 1998	Grolier Interactive
Reference/Ency	World Book 1997 Multimedia Encyclopedia	IBM
Reference/Ency	Encarta '97 Encyclopedia	Microsoft
Reference/Ency	Encarta 98 Encyclopedia	Microsoft
Reference/Ency	Compton's Interactive Encyclopedia 1998	The Learning Company
Reference/Ency.	Britannica OnLine	Encyclopeadia Britannica
Reference/Ency.	Ultimate Childrens' Encyclopedia	Learning Co.
Reference/Ency.	Collier's Encyclopedia 1998	Sierra Home
Science	Wide World of Animals	Creative Wonders
Science	Earth Quest	DK Multimedia
Science	Eyewitness Encyclopedia of Nature	DK Multimedia
Science	The Way Things Work 2.0	DK Multimedia
Science	FIND IT! SCIENCE	Follett Software
Science	Mayo Clinic Family Health Book	IVI Publishing
Science	Mammals Multimedia Encyclopedia	National Geographic Society
Science	Interactive Science CD-ROM	Steck Vaughn Company
Social Studies	Exegy	ABC-CLIO
Social Studies	ABC News Links	Creative Wonders
Social Studies	Eyewitness History of the World	DK Multimedia
Social Studies	World News CD-ROM	Facts on File
Social Studies	DISCovering U.S. History	Gale Publishing
Social Studies	DISCovering World History	Gale Publishing

Publisher's Addresses

Publisher	Street	City, State and Zip	Web Address
ABC-CLIO	P.O. Box 1911	Santa Barbara, CA 93116	market@abc-clio.com
Compton's NewMedia, Inc.	One Athenaeum Street	Cambridge, MA 02142	http://www.sierra.com
Creative Wonders	P. O. Box 9017	Redwood City, CA 94063	http://www.creativewonders.com
DK Multimedia	95 Madison Avenue	New York, NY 10016	http://www.dk.com
Ebsco Publishing	P.O Box 1943	Birmingham, AL 35201	http://www.epnet.com
Encyclopeadia Britannica	310 South Michigan Avenue	Chicago, IL 60604	http://www.eb.com
Facts on File	11 Penn Plaza	New York, NY 100001	http://www.facts.com
Facts on File News Services	11 Penn Plaza	New York, NY 100001	www.facts.com
Ferguson Publishing	299 West Madison St.	Chicago, IL 60606	
Follett Software	1391 Corporate Dr.	McHenry, IL 60050	http://www.fsc.follett.com
Gale Publishing	835 Penobscot Building	Detroit, MI 48226	http://www.gale.com
Grolier Educational	90 Sherman Turnpike	Danbury, CT 06816	http://www.grolier.com
Grolier Interactive	90 Sherman Turnpike	Danbury, CT 06816	http://www.grolier.com
H.W. Wilson	950 University Ave.	Bronx, NY 10452	http://www.hwwilson.com
IBM			http://www.worldbook.com
Infonautics	900 W. Valley Rd., Suite 1000	Wayne, PA 19087-1830	http://www.education.elibrary.com
IVI Publishing	7500 Flying Cloud Drive	Minneapolis, MN 55344	http://www.mayo.ivi.com
Learning Co.	6160 Summit Drive North	Minneapolis, MN 55430	http://www.learningco.com
Microsoft	PO Box 72368	Roselle, IL 60172-9900	htt://www.encarta.msn.com/
Mindscape	88 Rowland Way	Novata, CA 94945	http://www.mindscape.com/education.html
National Geographic Society	1145 17th St.	Washington, DC 20036	http://www.nationalgeographic.com
National Geographic Society	1145 17th St.	Washington, DC 20036	http://www.nationalgeographic.com
National Geographic Society	1145 17th St.	Washington, DC 20036	http://www.nationalgeographic.com
NewsBank	5020 Tamiami Trail Suite 110	Naples, FL 34103	http://infoweb.newsbank.com
Rand McNally	8255 North Central Park Ave.	Skokie, IL 60076-2970	http://www.randmcnally.com
Salem Press	580 Sylvan Avenue	Englewood Cliffs, NJ 07632	
Sierra Home	3380 146th Place, Suite 300	Bellview, WA 98007	http://www.sierra.com
SIRS, Inc.	P.O.Box 2348	Boca Raton, FL 33427	http://www.sirs.com
SoftKey International, Inc.	One Athenaeum St.	Cambridge, MA 02142	http://www.softkey.com
Steck Vaughn Company	P.O. Box 26015	Austin, TX 78755	http://www.steck-vaughn.com
The Learning Company	One Athenaeum Street	Cambridge, MA 02142	http://www.learningco.com
Time Warner Electronic Publishing	1271 Avenue of the Americas	New York, NY 10020	http://pathfinder.com/twep
UMI	300 North Zeeb Rd.	Ann Arbor, MI 48106	http://www.umi.com/

Index

Index